IN THE FRESH HEART OF THE FOREST

NOVEL WORKS

BY CAMILLE LEMONNIER

Copyright @ 2022
ISBN - 978-93-5478-825-3

Design and setting By
Zinc Read
Email- zincread@gmail.com

IN THE FRESH HEART
OF THE FOREST

I didn't know exactly how old I was: no one had taught me to count the years; and she herself could not get past the number ten when asked for hers.

So I said to him: "How old are you? " It was the first time. She answered me like everyone else:

- I'm ten years old.

The earth, for her, was ten years old as her own life and the life of all things around her. A mother had not marked on the wall in little lines the degree of her growth by counting: One, three, five, seven, and so on until the age she was now. There were nothing but horrible faces of misery on the horizon of his days, and no one had given him the family name.

She said to me: "Ten years"; and I laughed, because I, at least, could count to a hundred. It happened to me to have a hundred cherries or a hundred nuts, at the time of my marauding in the orchards. Then, always there had come a man armed with a pitchfork or a big dog who had put me to flight.

I leaned him against the trunk of a tree and with a sharp stone I marked the spot where the greatest height of his head reached. Then I passed the stone to him and in my turn I placed myself against the tree, saying to him:

- Make a mark for me in the bark as I did for you.

Only then did I turn around and saw that she was nearly one hand shorter than me. I was glad that there was this difference between us.

- See, I said, you only go that far and I almost reach that branch. I am also stronger than you, I have harder fingers. So I am your senior by several years.

And we were talking to each other like a brother and a sister. She looked at me sideways with her gray eyes, the eyes of a defiant little animal.

- If it is to fight me like the others that you speak thus, she said, I would have preferred not to go with you against the tree.

Once again I laughed, I laughed without meanness.

- No, little girl, it's not for what you think. Since I am the greatest, it is I who will beat them when they come.

The others had never spoken to him so quietly. Her gaze lit up through the tangle of her rusty linen hair. She came closer to me and said:

- Oh ! would you do that?

No one had spoken to me before that time with that confidence either. A wave passed, something unknown and serious, as when morning descends on the plain; and I said nothing, I couldn't find a word to express the strange feeling which suddenly linked my strength to its weakness. I only nodded a little bit for a while, answering her question; and now it was she who was laughing. I didn't know what made her laugh.

- Listen, she said, rummaging in the pocket of her skirt, if you're hungry, share this slice of bread with me. I found her at the door of a house over there.

She pointed to the city in the distance with her finger. I don't know how that morning, almost at the same time as I, she had come down to the country, so that we had found each other under the old tree. There were not yet any cherries in the orchards; the fruit barely began to tie; it was the time of year when we and nature seemed to be the same childhood age.

We sat down at the foot of the tree; she had drawn me by the hand and now she was breaking the slice of bread: she gave me half. It was the First Supper, like a little Passover for the poor who have nothing and who give themselves everything. So we sank our teeth into this loaf which once had been a light and fresh foam and which we had to break like a pebble. He thus came to us with the scornful remains of a sideboard, a feast. We were like city sparrows pecking in a heap for the joyous product of chance. When there were only a few crumbs left in the hollow of her skirt, she rolled them up in her hand and said:

- Take this again, since you are the tallest.

But I already thought that because of my size, it was right that I in turn gave him something. My eyes turned to the plain; she was dry and naked; heaps of rubble and cinders bloated it with little domes; at a fairly great distance a starving dog was gnawing at a bone which it clamped between its paws. He too was like us; he felt no disgust for the miserable remnant who appeased his hunger.

- You see, I said to this girl, we have to go further. Where we see flies, there will surely be something to eat.

We walked along the rubble; a chalky cloud rose from our feet; her feet were only a shred of espadrilles; sometimes she would turn away so as not to hurt herself in the broken bottles. Me, I went on my plantars; It had been nearly a week since my last bits of soles had come loose: it was an old pair of mismatched ankle boots, one with a delicate woman's foot, the other with the powerful toes of a ro-ro. Carefully I had worn them for part of the winter. We walked thus for nearly an hour; and at the end he passed big golden flies; all were heading with alert flight towards the cultivated areas. The city had disappeared behind us for a long time.

First we had ceased to see the tree under which we had broken bread and then in turn the tall chimneys sank into the fog of smoke. Now we felt as though we were freer, as if a weight had been lifted from our shoulders. Where we went, the earth was ours and there was only the two of us on the earth. However, words were lacking to express this feeling or another; and we didn't know if what we were feeling was joy. We could not say either of what sorrows before this moment we had been sad. She had appeared in that skinny suburb, with her red hair and skinny little legs under her skirt catch; she had come to the tree; we did not know each other and we recognized each other; me too, seeing her, I had taken a step towards the lonely old tree. There was no other at a great distance: he had grown in these hazardous confines like a poor man, like an ancestor who saw the trees of a forest die around him and survives them. We had risen like him in a desert of men. It was according to the order that we would meet one day, she and I, under its foliage, greened by spring.

Old tree forever unforgettable! the hail and the gusts had beaten you all winter and now you had a young hair of the sun. You cast shadows on our way, little wandering children, you who had no friendly shade on your bark. Oh ! she had come so pale, so weary with her little tense face, with the fever of her little body which had not been watched over by a mother! She and I were sick of the big smoky city and yet we did not know what either of us was sick of. We had a stomach and a heart like other men: we had never laughed and we had always been hungry. Now this little one was hitting the ground hard with her heels as if the world already belonged to her. She had, swinging her greasy little petticoat with mud and soot, a light dance rhythm. And she was laughing

She said to me strangely:

- Wasn't there once a town there? Wasn't there a boy and a girl who one day went to each other through the countryside?

The city had hardly faded on the horizon and yet she spoke of it as of a distant event. It was already around our small leaps across the plain like the air in disuse on which an ancient legend is sung. It was so long since the city was behind us, so long that we no longer knew who this young boy and this little girl were! And now we were walking through a green and rich land. An army of flies were our ambassadors as when it comes to a king and a queen. They went by great flights; birds welcomed us to our new kingdom.

- Oh ! see, I say, there are so many trees and we don't know what's behind it!

She wet her finger and held it out in the wind, then brought it to her mouth.

- It's sweet, she said, it's sweet like milk.

Neither she nor I had ever gotten this far; the cherry orchards were on the other side of town. Our light feet ran, leaving thousands of footprints in the dust, like the footsteps of a people who came in line before us in this land of tall foliage. And finally we trod the velvet meadows; a stream sinua; I had only to bend down to pick a greasy and peppery watercress in handfuls. She came and sat down beside me; she untied the ropes that held the sneakers to her toes; and then, with a shudder of pleasure, she let her feet sink over the water. Sometimes, laughing, I waved with my heels in the current: eddies bubbled up, blurring the reflection of her legs.

As we remained leaning over the stream, a great light rose from the bottom of this limpid wave; and we recognized our faces. It seemed to us that we were seeing each other for the first time.

- You are much more beautiful than I thought, she said.

And I tell him:

- You have the whole sky in your hair.

Yet we were only poor little crossroads lives, sisters of hardworking stray dogs. But here we are, until then we had soaked our feet in the fetid mud of the gullies, scavenging on the edge of the gloomy suburbs populated with dilapidated and pustular homes. All our days had been Sundays without Mass in a parish of crime and misery, inhabited by lamentable crowds with mouths stinking of curse and alcohol. And now we were breathing freely under the great limitless sky, far from men. A blue wave washed our cool feet; we had not yet tasted the sweetness of such a truce.

Ah! we had already been on the march for so many years! It seemed to us that we had always walked with our weary feet of children and neither of us knew where it came from: a hand had pushed us and then we did not stop. That is why, feeling the soft and cool earth beneath us, we remained amazed and happy. We were in the blue space another boy and another girl who did not yet know the joy of the world; and before that time we had not known the color of the sky either.

He undulated us in his silk folds as the little river bathed our feet: he displayed over our nakedness the sumptuous hangings of a palace. The wind in our ears sounded like music. Words failed us to tell each other the beauty of wonders. However, as it is always to heaven that the virgin man brings back his impulses, I had said ingenuously: "You have all the sky in your hair. "

It was the afternoon. The sun was scorching our red skins: gold was flowing in our blood. We left, following our shadow on the path. She hopped on one foot, pushing a stone in front of her with her toe. Once she started running so far that I wanted to yell at her. Only then did I think that I didn't even know the name by which he was called. I tell him :

- Take a look: you came and I still don't know your name.

She showed me her skinny little arms.

- I was always shaking when I was little. Mama once called me "Frilotte" and then everyone called me that. There you go, I never knew what it was like to be hot.

She spoke of this part of her life as a very old thing. I was laughing ; I did not feel at the moment how sad it was that she had known only a name so unhuman.

- You, you are Frilotte, I said to him, and I am Little Old Man.

I don't remember who once gave me this nickname out of mockery of my taciturn and lonely mood. I was neither ashamed nor hurt. It was indifferent to me, after all, like life, like the idea that some creature had given birth to me cursing me. She could have laughed as I myself had laughed; his name was no more ridiculous than mine; the same irony weighed on our lives. She looked at me seriously.

- Oh ! she said, we call you Old Man, you who have eyes like a child!

I shrugged and she thought of something else. We had not yet learned to wonder about ourselves. We were wrecks rolled away by the flood of ages; the crowds had been our family.

However she began to yawn and said to me:

- I'm hungry.

It was the first time and it was the word of our whole life. Every hour of the day, our body cried out to us: "I carry you, I yield to your wishes and you do nothing to repair the wear and tear of my strength. A grindstone is spinning in me. Angry dogs are gnawing at me. Feed me or I will deny you the service of your members. It was the same cry which relentlessly relaunched the maddened distress of the human packs through the streets of the city. We had always heard him: he woke us up on the flagstones where we stretched out overwhelmed sleep; and behold, he was coming up from us, now, into the divine hour.

So I, unconsciously, undergo the feeling of a duty towards this child who has come in my footsteps. I was not sad; sadness is so much the natural state of the destitute that it remains at the bottom of life like cloudy water which does not overflow. I tell Frilotte to wait for me. I started running, I followed the flies under the trees, always further. They entered a stable, and next to it I saw a house. I knew by what words to evoke charity; here and there I had held out my hand from the back of a porch when luck did not help me in my precarious little jobs. In summer, I went to pick grasses and blueberries around the orchards; I would then come back to offer them to passers-by. Or else I would open the car doors in front of the restaurants at night; but great violent thugs and agile sly old men contested me for this coveted post. I also fell back towards the covered markets and worked to sweep the tile oozing with tide or juicy rotten fruit. These were my best profits.

I knocked on the threshold; an elderly woman came dragging her clogs.

"Frilotte is hungry," I told him decisively. If you had a little piece of bread?

The grandmother was in a happy mood; she turned to a young mother who, in the back of the room, was rocking a child.

- Frilotte! she said. This one must surely be as funny as him!

They both laughed without malice. The pitiful old woman took a quarter of brown bread from the hutch, cut it in half, then between the portions crushed a drizzle of butter. I don't know if I had ever experienced such joy before. I flew to my friend; I put the bread in his hands, saying:

- Have you ever eaten butter?

His eyes were shining; the old instinct of distrust reappeared; she looked at me sideways as if she feared that after giving her the bread, I would take it again. I shook my head.

- It's yours, you can give me what you want.

She gave a little cry of a wild beast, like the beings who have learned to speak badly. Wow ! Wow ! she said, expressing very frank joy. She inhaled the sour smell of rye for a long time; and then, as she had done the first time under the tree, she divided the bread with her little brown hands. We had gone towards tall poplars; we sat down in their shadow. She never finished licking the butter; it was the color of the sun. When the beautiful yellow layer had all melted in her mouth, she only began to bite deeply into the thickness of the stalk. Yes, the city was far away.

A chill rose as we finished this tasty meal. Neither of us had thought that there would come a time when we would have to make up our minds to return to the path of the old tree. The plain reddened with oblique rays: I stuck out my finger towards the smoky city.

- Hey, Frilotte, will we go back there?

She answered me:

- If you go back, I'll go with you.

I always carried a pebble in my pocket. When I had to decide whether the luck would come from the right path or the left path, I pulled the stone and threw it in the air. This pebble, moreover, gave me the illusion of possessing, like the rich, something which weighed the weight of money. The humble poor children have a helpful ingenuity towards themselves. I could have taken the pebble this time again: throwing it in front of me, I would have tossed or tails fixed our destiny. Frilotte's quiet decision gave me confidence in myself. With a resolute mind I say:

- We'll go that way.

I was showing him the road ahead of us. Now we were both full of hatred for the city.

Oh ! the pig! the pig! the horrible stepmother who had always taken the bread out of our teeth, who had quenched our thirsts with her milkless breast! We had shivered there in the winter and roasted there in the summer, naked, homeless, staving off our hunger with scraps that we disputed with the dogs. But they got up earlier than we did: almost always, when we came to browse through the heaps, they had already passed. I was the Old Man who, from the days of my infancy, dragged the world's misery after him. I couldn't tell what feeling made me so old that I never seemed to have been young. I was perhaps the extension of ancient races that had suffered from hunger and cold before me. She too, this little flower of the pavement that could only count to ten, would have been unable to sum up his distress. But this was a living essence; she had a morning gaiety in her light bird wings. She laughed as the wind laughs in a sick room when the windows are open. Her mobile little woman's spirit danced in front of her on the path. She turned one last time to where the towers had disappeared on the horizon and spat away with an angry pout. And then immediately she thought only of having fun with her new life. She turned one last time to where the towers had disappeared on the horizon and spat away with an angry pout. And then immediately she thought only of having fun with her new life. She turned one last time to where the towers had disappeared on the horizon and spat away with an angry pout. And then immediately she thought only of having fun with her new life.

- Say, Old Man, will there be cherries there in the summer? Will there be lukewarm haystacks to sleep in? Will there be slices of fine buttered bread when we want to eat?

His hands clapped with a clear noise. She breathed in the scent of the grass, her nose in the wind, like a little heifer. The soul of the earth entered her. I thought, "There won't be dogs up there until daybreak." "

The sun went down peacefully; the sky on our step was sowing roses; the wind had retained a little of the heat of the day. There appeared farms, thatched roofs, flowered fences. The grasses and sand cooled our feet. We then walked along a large wood and all evening had not fallen. A little light paled our faces; we were close to each other like little shadows; again we thought we hadn't known each other yet. Then this remainder of day died out, the blue night enveloped us. She said to me singularly:

- Is it really you, Old Man, who is there near me?

I was saying :

- Is it really you, little Frilotte?

Our names were very sweet to us like the butter on the sandwich and we could no longer see the mouths saying them. She sank her hand into mine. I had not yet felt the warmth of the flesh in the other girls. Frightful little monkeys had bitten me to the point of blood; I myself had pulled their hair by handfuls. The feeling hadn't been any different from my brawls with the boys.

So it was a new and deep thing, the softness of his hand in my hand. The cherries alone had the moisture of that warm little skin. We would have gone like that to the end of the world. A great silence fell: children's voices far away were silent; the barking of a dog had also dragged a little while; there was nothing on us except at night a wood with small leaves stirred, with the light cracking of twigs like a little more silence. An unreal appearance fluffed the shapes, cool silks of fluid shadow flowing. We no longer spoke to each other, all we had to hear each other was the warmth of our hands, one in the other.

We were not afraid: the city nights with their flashing streetlamps and their drunken groans, the heavy darkness like mortuaries after livid twilights, the damp black of the streets battered by howling gusts and crisscrossed with prowling watches had exhausted in us the shivers of fear. Rather, it was a feeling of trust and security as if we were relying on an unknown vigilance to preserve ourselves. Someone softly seemed to speak in the night, someone who perhaps had closed their lids by day and was rocking the trees; and no one had taught us God. We thus arrived at the edge of a clearing.

There she said to me:

- I'm tired, Old Man.

His hand had been heavy on my arm for a little while. His feet too grated the path without courage. My best nights there were those I spent, lying on the joists of the great iron bridges, over the dark quiet river. It flowed with its eternal stream and without noise. Towards morning heavy wagons passed; the whole frame was trembling; I was rocked as in a storm. Frilotte, she slept in the burning and fetid odor of the slums where a human eddy was piled up. Sometimes it fell behind an embankment, against a door, near a cellar window. Neither of them yet knew the tender night of the woods.

In the evening of the clearing, an oak like a church stood up. His foot was bulging with monstrous toes, felted with moss. I laughed as I felt the softness of this bed, soft like a little bird's down.

"See, Frilotte, if you wouldn't be well here," I said.

She answered something I couldn't understand, and she let herself fall between the thick ribs of the tree. However, I, looking at the splendid sky above her, I still say in a low voice:

- They lit all the candles up there.

I didn't know who I was talking about; obscure words arise from the depths of the ignorant, which nevertheless have a meaning. Thousands of stars riddled the light foliage of the oak; all the holes in the sky, through the young spring of the leaves, had a quiet pallor of night-lights. On Christmas nights, there were lighted trees in the windows like that. But Frilotte no longer made a movement. She had folded her bare legs under her petticoat; his eyelids had fallen. A breath passed.

- Good evening, Old Man.

A poor boy once told me that too. This one was still coughing. He had come to sleep with me in a cellar near the river. I slipped into it, sliding between the air vents. That evening he tenderly said goodnight to me. And then he never woke up again.

I was lying at the foot of the oak, in the cool down of the earth with a strange life in me. My hands caressed soft and lively fabrics, like flesh. The trees also lived, and the stars, and all the depth of the wood. I had there for the first time the presentiment of a mystery around the creature. It was just an idea that came from the beauty of the night and descended in my blood. And I hardly knew my blood from seeing it dripping from my injured limbs. I knew much less of my life's relationship with the eternal meaning of things. Who ever would have told me about God and the universe? But the earth beneath me was pulsating; endless rumors rose from the clearing; the sap rustled in the arterioles like saliva on my lips, like blood in my veins.

I had pressed my ear to the oak; it vibrated in all its height and a sound wave ran under its bark. My subtle little savage hearing thought I recognized the noise of the city when you can hear it from afar in the evenings, with its chariot rolling on the flagstones, its brass and drums music, its buzzing like a beehive.

My fear suddenly trembled as in front of a prodigy. I would have liked to wake up Frilotte, shout at him:

- Little girl ! the earth has a heart like you and me!

The first men to enter the forests must have experienced this feeling of religious terror.

I laid my head near that of Frilotte; I no longer had a movement; and a light, deep noise also rose from his life, his sleep made music like a big fly, like the breathing of this nocturnal land. A calm tide always rose and fell; I watched her tenderly palpitating mouth under the stars. Like mine, she had shouted insults; she had repeated the execrable words which, on a child's lips, have the torn redness of a wound. Now she was quivering softly like the heart of a rose. A numbness seized me: I felt myself pass out lukewarm in the heat of his blood.

And then it was our first morning. Almost at the same time we opened our eyes. Drops of light rained down from the branches, rolled down our faces. Our flesh was wet with dawn. What astonishment for both of them! She looked at me with clear eyes of wonder. It seemed to me that it was another girl who was near me. In the cool hour she no longer had the same pale forehead that had come to the tree the day before. Her mouth too was another flower of blood, fiery and mobile. And again, in the virgin landscape, it was as if we had not seen each other yet. She was resting on the moss bed like an air spirit, like a subtle form of dream. I looked at her with young eyes, washed with light.

- Is that you, Frilotte?

And before I had never smiled.

- Yes, she said, it's me, but is it you, Little Old Man, who touches me with your hand?

A light wind blew over our eyes. The clearing was smoking; a blue shadow fell from the trees and cut like a prow the silvery lake of vapors. The sun was crackling, bright and bold. A cuckoo, in the distance of the wood, sang three times.

- Oh ! she said, someone called us.

- No, it's a bird, little girl.

However, I did not know what this bird was. She and I only knew the street sparrows; and we ourselves were now like sparrows that left the city and came to the big trees. A thousand sources rose from the ground, continuous, deep. The heart of the earth beat with great bangs. From moment to moment life was rising; it rolled like a sea; and the same hand which had slid the hinges of the night reopened the locks of the day.

Again I rested my ear against the bark of the oak. He snored like a millstone; all the wood seemed to quiver in its magnificent life, as, in the breast of a king, the whole soul of a people. I was no longer the same fearful child who had trembled in the mystery of the shadows.

"Listen, Frilotte," I cried. He too lives like us.

She didn't know what I meant. And then a drunken joy passed through me. Crying, I hugged the big tree like a friend, like a brother. A cloud of birds flew away, a woodpecker in the distance neighed. Every sound of the forest was a wonder; but above all the cuckoo charmed us. Again he struck three knocks. Over there at the watchmaker's we had seen a black bird come up to the edge of a door, uttering three jerky hiccups. She tells me :

- Let's go where this bird cries.

We walked for a while in the damp thyme. Each step of which we tread the soft ground gave off green scents. We called out: Hello! Hello ! And three more times the bird answered, but each time its voice seemed to recede into the depth of the wood.

The thickets thickened: a wild melee opened and closed in our path, and other birds now came to greet us at the tips of the branches. There were some who seemed to be dripping crystal water with the tip of their beaks; every drop tingled clear and fresh. Finches resembled the little musicians who go off to play the violin in front of the open-air cafes on Sundays. And then the oriole hissed; he had only four notes, always the same; it was wet, mocking and tender. There was also in town a flageolet player who, with his fingers on the holes in the sonorous wood, made this melodious noise. Sometimes jays bitterly cried.

- Oh ! said Frilotte, I think I hear the old woman bickering with Mama.

The joy of the wood passed through us. With patience I tried to modulate the four notes of the oriole. Our laughter was a bird song to our mouths: it rose from us as the smell of thyme rose from the ground trodden by our feet. He was the analogy of our little elementary souls with the mirth of the morning. In the past we had laughed with a rather nasty laugh, at the tip of our teeth, like biting in self-defense. We were then the little beasts of the human thicket; we had not yet heard the laughter of the wind in the trees.

However, Frilotte suddenly began to chatter his teeth and again the hunger had returned. Like the wolf she had come out of the woods and now she was pouncing on us. It was the same bark as the other mornings, as every day of our life. We took a handful of green herbs; their acrid juice twitched us; we tried in vain to chew bark. So, with pale eyes, she began to talk about the beautiful buttered bread of the grandmother.

- Ah! I said, if only we could find our way back to this house!

We had not lost the courage; we were accustomed to deserve our uncertain daily subsistence through patient toil. We tried to orient ourselves. Our bare feet did not stop hitting the ground quickly. At the end, Frilotte let himself down.

"Go alone, Old Man," she said weakly. I will stay here.

But immediately after, clinging to my hands:

- No, no, Old Man, carry me. What would I be doing here alone without you? I don't want to die in this horrible wood.

So I took her in my arms and carried her a little while; but in my turn I felt my strength running out. I was very overwhelmed. How ironic this sun and all this joy of trees and birds over our agony! We were there close to each other, squeezing our stomachs with our hands. Then, crushing it with all the weight of our body on the ground, we tried to suffocate the hungry beast that cried inside us. In town at least, the dogs sometimes hadn't eaten everything when we passed. Nature was more terrible than men.

As once again I turned on my stomach, I saw a line of large black and shiny insects advance. They rowed slowly under the grass and seemed to be heading towards carnage, towards a land of rich prey. Having taken a few steps, I saw a dead wood pigeon at the foot of a tree, moving under the assault of their black legions. A rhythmic life throbbed under the wings; the down of the feathers gently undulated in slow and broad continuous shocks. However, no one had told these voracious insects that there was a tasty debris there: their sure instinct had guided them and now by the hundreds they were feeding on the wood pigeon.

A poor boy, a primitive being binds his ideas with more spontaneity than the civilized person of the cities. I say to Frilotte:

- There are nests in the trees. If I stay a little while without coming back, cry like the bird three times.

Like the cat on the lookout, I slipped into the woods, listening to the murmur emanating from the tall foliage. I avoided the crackle of twigs, the rustle of dry leaves, and always looked above me into the green thickness of the branches. A deadly force was binding my nerves. My heart was pounding hard. I certainly lived there for a long time. At the end a summit stirred; a stir of frightened motherhood dragged on for a moment, and then fell back on a quiver of young wings. The instinct of the wild animal, the frenzied taste of the prey immediately darted. To enjoy a procession or watch a regiment parade, I had climbed the candelabra many times, knotted my knees to the smooth plane trees, with the agile suppleness of a monkey. But the tree, rough and vast, this time defied the embrace of my too short limbs. A young beech, fortunately by the top, joined one of the large branches of this ancestor of the wood. I hugged him in my arms, my hocks grabbed and with the strength of the kidneys I began to pull myself up. Soon I reached the tall branches; they bent, frail and tender; only their extremities brushed against the powerful veins of the oak. Now the fear of the nest was rumbling; the male inflated the feather; the female had huddled the brood widely under her outstretched wings. I could clearly see under its belly the sharp yellow beaks of the tumultuous little ones. only their extremities brushed against the powerful veins of the oak. Now the fear of the nest was rumbling; the male inflated the feather; the female had huddled the brood widely under her outstretched wings. I could clearly see under its belly the sharp yellow beaks of the tumultuous little ones. only their extremities brushed against the powerful veins of the oak. Now the fear of the nest was rumbling; the male inflated the feather; the female had huddled the brood widely under her outstretched wings. I could clearly see under its belly the sharp yellow beaks of the tumultuous little ones.

Then a cold decision tied my will. A sure momentum alone could overcome the space which separated me from the nest. I impressed the beech with stronger oscillations and finally launched myself. I thought I was falling from the height of a sky. A crash of twigs cracked; light and shadow split apart, with a long noise of split silks. The whole oak was shaken as if by a violent gust; and I, elastic and supple, my eyes clear in this prodigious leap, I rolled among a sea of foliage. A branch, twisted like a cable, stopped me, I hung on; and a flight now whirled; the wood pigeons pierced me with pecks. But already, with a savage clamor, I had torn off the nest and sank it against my flesh.

I let myself fall from branch to branch; and then, aiming at the next young beech, I opened my hands and with a bold leap again plunged into the green abyss. Foliage cushioned the fall; I rolled, without too much difficulty, over the mossy humus. Grains drizzled on my hands; a large gash scratched my cheek; the blood of the little wood pigeons smeared my chest.

There was there a feeling of fierce pride such as the old men of the woods must have felt. I had played my life in a heroic act. I had equaled myself to my will; I believe that instinct spoke thus in me, because my feelings could not yet be expressed. I shouted three times, but I no longer knew how the cuckoo sang: I uttered the furious clamor of a king. And over there, a weak voice answered me.

- See, I said, throwing the nest at his feet, these beasts were alive just now.

She handled them, still warm and throbbing. Bright roses bloomed on her cheeks; his nostrils were pounding. She was against me with shining eyes, a fierce and tender joy of life, uttering her savage cry.

Soon the light feather flew under his fingers. I gathered wood, dry leaves; I took my stone; I made the spark come out. The fire sparkled clear and pink: it rose under the oaks like the little soul of a brood. And between the knotted legs of the wood pigeons, I had slipped a scion that we pushed aside or brought together according to the intensity of the flame. The flesh turned golden. An aroma of grilling mingled with the smell of incense from burnt wood. With long saliva we watched the cooking finish. How could a young boy like me have suspected the reason for the appalling attraction which the smell of sizzling meat in the fire gives off to man? The blood of a lifetime on the grill is more delectable than the flavor of generous fruit, than the scent of freshly kneaded bread. Barely, for having sniffed it on the threshold of the rotisseries, I knew the pungent peppery smell of meat. And now at the smell of that little flesh that had palpitated and bled a pink juice, my lips were lengthening on their own.

The predator instinct dominated us: we slashed the tender threads at the tips of the canines. We crushed the young bones of the threads of the old oak between our molars. It was left to us like an overwhelmed intoxication which made us sleep, happy and sated, a long hour of sleep.

Upon awakening, thirst in turn tortured us; this flaming meat made our throats hot. But the grass was hot; we sucked leaves; they gave us only a momentary refreshment. We regretted the clear stream: we had lost the way for ever. Between him and us, like a wheel the great trees were turning.

A scarlet forge lit up in the depths: the sun rolled like a head under hammers. We were in a thick thicket, in the very heart of the immense wood. An illusion had thrown us among the brambles and thorns reddened by the setting sun; from a distance we thought we saw purple fruit. Splinters bruised our legs; a piece of Frilotte's skirt got caught in the claws of the thicket. She swore like a drunken old woman; I went, tapping with a stick in front of me, cautiously. Nimble and long forms suddenly sprang up, a frightened and graceful thrill of light, almost flying lives, in the slenderness of their flight. What animal thus could hold out of the flexible greyhound, of the ardent and sensitive horse? There was indeed a garden of animals in the city; their fury filled the evenings of the neighborhood. Those at least had a name in my memory, a name that sometimes came to the mouths of the most ignorant, lion, tiger, wolf. And once, hoisted to the crest of a wall, I could see, beyond the fence, massive fleeces and jerky footsteps. But no one had ever told us about the innocent deer.

- Oh ! she whispered to me, I'm afraid, Old Man.

I twisted the stick. The pride of carnage was in me for having tasted blood.

'If there is one more,' I cried, 'I'll kill her.

- Would you really do it? she says.

His nostrils were throbbing like the last time.

The bramble tree a little further deepened; a soft and green area rippled on the slopes of a valley where night was already falling. We had a cry. A clear rivulet streamed from a spring and meandered through the depths. We drew this miraculous water with our palms; it filtered with our fingers in threads of silver; we were never done drinking, and a deep sweetness flowed with it into our thirsty chests. We would have stayed there for hours, divinely refreshed by the delicious scenery.

We followed the light current; the trees receded; a pool, a motionless slumber of water softened with a violet shadow. Slowly the sky began to grow pale; starlight, like drops of milk, streamed from the night's breasts. So two children, holding hands, went up the slopes and they neither laughed nor talked to each other, very pure and happy in the goodness of the shadows. They had come from the horrible town, with their guts dying of hunger; they had taken each other's hands and had walked in front of them. A free life was already paying them with their long exhausted distresses. And neither had learned to put their fingers together; yet a religious soul was on their mouths.

She hugged me.

'Old man,' she said, 'once there was a church.

There she was, she was telling the truth: it was there like the church she was talking about, but still in the city, after a little while, a solemn man chased us away, sounding his halberd on the flagstones.

Night entered our wild souls like a sleeping bag, like fresh spring water. A slow breeze rose, the wind of a breath like the brushing of feathers and silks. It was so long since we had stopped suffering from the other evil life, me sleeping under the roaring decks of bridges, you in foul slums reeked by the smell of sewage and alcohol! An aroma of saps and gums sweetened our lips. With each stroke we thought we were sucking in the enormous green soul of the wood. We had the virgin senses of two little fauns listening to the mystery.

The shadows quivered over agile hikes, slow, furtive glides. Pursuits fled through the paths. In the thickness of the oaks ran enamored hunts of squirrels. And light cries, sometimes the longer moan of a wounded animal, mingled with the cracking of branches, the rustling of foliage, the muffled beating of wings. A continuous rumor hung out, the throbbing of lives near and far lurking in the woods. Suddenly an owl fleece choked, followed by a small rattle of agony and wood pigeons sighed like happy lovers. Almost immediately a gallop cut through the night; precipitated hooves bounced towards the pond. I saw the slender, quivering grace of long, female-eyed animals.

Frilotte shivered, snuggled up in my arms.

- I assure you, Old Man, they are not animals like the others.

The soft air fell silent; the great night of the woods dozes off; there was like a velvet finger that brushed our eyelids. We fell asleep in the cool soul of the earth. And then again the morning awoke. We shivered under the height of the trees. We never stop admiring the wonder of their enormous trunks above us, so small.

Days passed. We were counting the hours by the curve of the sun. Six times he had risen to a clear sky, flowered with roses. Immediately life rose; the cuckoo, with its little taps, gave the signal. This one was the morning singer, posted behind the gates of the day. Then the oriole played his little tune; the swooning moan of the wood pigeons dragged on; the woodpecker snorted with the neighing of a colt; the bitter clamor of the jays grilled; and we also recognized the strident forest of the magpie and the hoarse blow of the plane of the crows. We invented names to distinguish them from each other and some charmed us, others stimulated in us a taste for hunting and fighting.

As we slipped into the green valley, we were going to watch the deer drinking from the pond. In small leaps they climbed the slopes and in our turn we descended towards the source to drink there and soak our feet. I no longer thought of the murder; they were like us, gentle and confident souls, in the peace of nature. They got used to our faces; we could approach them at a short distance; their fresh luminous eyes followed us and were no longer worried.

The hour of hunger drew me back to the tall foliage. The flesh of the wood pigeon was precious to us, with a less pungent flavor than the magpie and the jay. Instinct taught me how, by twisting my shred of jacket and throwing it along the tree in front of me, I could surely pull myself up to the nests. Wow ! Wow ! she cried. Then the fire was lit, we innocently ate winged life. I did not yet dare to touch the other beings in the woods. And it was the month of love; drops of sap rained down from the leaves; the bark coagulated the hot sweat of the resins. A few essences oozed a peppery gum which burned our lips; the heart of the oaks, nourished with virgin blood, rang like a drum. However, we were still ignorant of the agitation of our flesh; we hadn't noticed a different gender.

Around the tenth night, the moon changed. A fine rain wet our alarm clock; it sizzled on the mosses, it streamed from the leaves with clear music which at first amused us. The cuckoo that morning sounded hoarse, and we no longer heard the merry birds of the woods. Only the jays and crows continued to quarrel harshly in the mournful silence. Towards noon, the rain thickened: its dull and continuous noise resembled the distant march of a crowd. All other rumors had died down. A heavy, gray air tinned the day. Like the birds, we had lost our gaiety.

We had to vary our stations under the oaks; the downpour visited our shelters. Necessity then made me industrious. I went into the thicket to cut the straightest branches. I juxtaposed them, squeezing them together with sprigs of elbow tree. This wattle provided us with a simulacrum of a roof; I fixed it on two stakes, keeping a slope for the flow of water. Small branches then braided formed the walls. As the cold had taken hold of us, I lit a fire of twigs near the hut. We thus had an encampment in the heart of the woods, like the foundations of a young city. And it rained from dawn until night for five days.

The trees, under the great fruitful rain, shone a full and rich green. Germs flourished, a chilly grace of small pale corollas stared at the deep layers. The aromas also more subtly rose from the drained soil. One morning the birds began to sing again. Days of cool light golden the foliage. We left our hut; we walked for a long time through the wood.

One evening she said to me:

- So think about that. Mama would sometimes take me in her knees and kiss me.

I, believing that she regretted the other life, my heart ached with annoyance.

- Well, I said, if you want, we'll go back to town. You will go find this Mama.

My voice was shaking: I would have beaten her if she had said yes.

- No, she said, it's not what you think, Old Man. Mama always came back with men. When she was drunk there was nothing good to expect from her, but then she would become very tender again; she was crying and begging my forgiveness. If only you wanted to stroke my hair a bit like she did!

I didn't think she would ever ask me this thing. She had curled up against me and now she was taking my hands, pressing them gently to her forehead.

- Oh ! it's so good, your hands, Little Old Man!

I lent myself a little time to this game and then I went through the woods. I was not angry, it was something unique in me that I did not know. When I returned, she was sleeping peacefully, her arms crossed over her chest.

Another time, we had left in the morning. We went hand in hand, swinging our arms. Dull thoughts stirred me and I said to him:

- Think about this. There are men who work in the fields. They turn the earth, they sow the wheat. They go with the oxen and the horses. These are better than me and you.

She frowned and shouted:

- They are not free like us!

Oh ! she was saying something true there and yet I could not agree with her. The insect, the tree and the spring work in their own way; they do a necessary work like the plowman and the sower. I had arms and hands and they were useless to me. Thus the law reappeared, the destiny which dedicates man to work; and I wasn't reasoning, it was a confused instinct that made me regret something I could have done. A poor boy's heart is closer to humanity than others.

So I walked beside Frilotte without saying anything, moved by things without words, while she laughed madly and danced under the trees. Suddenly I stopped and shouted wildly:

- They eat bread, those who work!

Here, the ideas were tied and now they burst forth in this cry which was that of the races, the very wish of life. Yes, these sowed the earth; the rye and the wheat rose from their sweat, and then they kneaded the light grind: the bread paid for their sorrows.

She looked at me very pale, her eyes sick.

- Oh ! she said, breaking a crust of bread with her teeth!

We would have given our hut to be like them and savor the sour smell of hot rye. He spent a sadness under the trees, the trampled thyme ceased to rejoice us. Our saliva had the bitter taste of desire.

It was an easterly, dry and sharp midday. Hunger had made us seek our food far away; we were starting to miss the nests. Soon the thickets became sparse; there were only beeches left; their colonnade rose and fell on slopes.

- Oh ! she said, would this finally be the limit of this wood?

We dared not look at each other; all the free joy of our life was forgotten; there was nothing left but the anguish of the unknown of the world which was beyond the beeches. Now a pungent smell of mud and coal blew towards us. I recognized the smell of baked brick: it lived in the cool buildings, in the houses under construction where so often, in the sand and the mortar, had lodged my harsh winter nights.

- Believe me, I say, let's not go any further. There was also that smell to the city.

She started without hearing me and in my turn I started to run, pushed by a force. Soon a bluish smoke enveloped us in light flakes. Trees darted like golden barrels from the misty edges. An immense plain stretched out. With mute astonishment, we gazed near the burning ovens at the huts of a brickwork camp.

The sun was setting straight, it was noon. Men were sleeping, almost naked, their stomachs flat against the threshing floor. Some, squatting on their backs, cut large quarters of bread with their knives and held them to their teeth.

These continually moved their jaws like grindstones. They half-closed their eyes in the joy of savoring the heavy, fragrant loaf. It seemed to us that a long time of our life had passed since we had ceased to see beings made in our image. Women then came out of the huts and brought jars full of black brew. There were also children; the youngest were already helping in the common work: the clay was sticky to their skins and they had the agile feet of deer in the woods. Together they were the tribe of the soil kneaders who skim the countryside and go before the next step of the city builders.

A dog saw us and barked; we became once again the fierce little essences revived by the fear of men in society. A rapid flight threw us back into the woods. But again, after some time, a strange sympathy brought us back. Part of the team was spoiling the blond clay that the women soaked with the water from the seils. A coming and going of wheelbarrows carried the substance thus prepared, soft enough for shaping. And standing in front of the table, the chef, a supple and nervous old man, received the dough, inserted it into molds like waffle irons, leveled the boxes with a skilful stroke of the plane, then passed them to the nimble children who had them. poured out on the ground powdered with golden sand. We watched without speaking to each other the harmonious beauty of this work which was still unknown to us.

The mysterious allure brought us back the next day. I would have liked to run alongside them, dragging loads of clay, feeling the warmth of their skin against mine. And once again we were there, the body pushed forward on our fists, looking out over the plain.

- Oh ! she said, breads!

One of the huts was gaping, and with her finger she pointed to a row of large loaves of bread on the wall. His sharp teeth were quivering; I, too, gazed longingly at the powerful golden crusts. I did not think that this bread had been painfully earned by sacred work. I looked at her and then I looked at the big ruddy wheels. His sick, choppy laugh encouraged me.

Cautiously I crawled out of the woods, I slipped to the threshold. A half-light fell from the joists and I could only see the light spot of the loaves. I stretched out my hand; an arm fell; I hadn't noticed that a man was lying on a straw litter near the door. He stood up, dragged me through the camp and over there this mean girl was now fleeing behind the trees. The tribe ran to the cries of the man; there was a commotion, frenzied gestures; they all cursed me. But suddenly one of the bricklayers let out a cry of pain and anger. Like a little wolf, a girl had come out of the woods and planted her canines in her hand. Blood in his mouth, Frilotte braved them, uttering his war cry. Wow

! Wow ! Her cowardly little soul had awakened, fearless and violent.

The chef strode in, the agile and supple old man who maneuvered the waffle iron over there. He split the group, grabbed my neck, pulled her herself by the arm. And he had his gaze straight into a harsh face.

- Who are you, you who steal the bread?

I looked him straight in the eye, shrugging my shoulders.

- I do not know.

- Where do you come from ?

I indicated a point in space behind me.

- And that one, say, is she your sister?

I didn't think he would have asked me that question. I opened my mouth and then clenched my teeth, not knowing what to say. But suddenly Frilotte shouted strangely:

- I am his wife.

These people laughed; the chief alone, under his furrowed brow, did not laugh and looked her deep in the eyes. She had spoken to him with the fierce pride of a little town savage who made no distinction between fraternal life and the other. Gently he asked her:

- How old are you ?

- I have four sizes in the tree less than Petit Vieux.

Now I was laughing with the men who were there. However, the wife of the one who had suddenly been bitten in the hand approached, a stone in her hand.

- Believe me, said the chef, take a loaf of bread and cut it in half. This boy and this girl have committed no other crime than to be hungry.

The woman therefore let the stone roll; she stepped under the thatch and then came back, bringing half of one of the large loaves of bread. He had taken his large hand off my shoulder, he took the bread; and now he was addressing me as one of his own, with a fatherly and grave face.

- The little ones you see around me are the sons of my sons. There are some who are not ten years old. Yet they are already working and they are helping us earn the bread we eat. You prefer to go into houses and steal the bread you did not deserve. Now, if you and her are hungry, take this. You may then want to work like us. In that case, come back tomorrow. There are never enough arms to bake the brick and activate the ovens.

Without doubt this one knew the feminine versatility. That's why he didn't turn to this little girl; and he was before me like a man talking to a man. I listened to him, stirred with a great inner movement.

- Now come on, he said.

The women pushed us out of the camp and he walked back to the table.

- See, she said, laughing, they are working hard and we are free. This bread will seem much better to us.

The loaf was fresh and smelled of the ripe field; we were digging our teeth into it furiously. It was still life, though it was no longer blood and bones, like the prey I stole from trees, and it foamed in our mouths, light and golden. A heat swelled my heart; I thought of the old man: no man had yet spoken to me with such severe kindness. If I had been alone, I would have returned to the camp. However, I was wary of Frilotte. I hissed between my teeth and then said indifferently:

- Wouldn't you have wanted to have a father like this man too?

She stopped eating, looked at me right under my nose, shaking her red hair:

- All men, it's you now for me, Old Man, she cried with a real joy of possession, with a burst of personal and wild life.

Where did this little animal girl get such strange ideas? Our flesh still remained obscure to us and already she spoke to me like a woman, with an imperious tenderness in the creases of her eyebrows. The male force immediately rebelled, the virgin instinct of defense, as if it had made an attempt on the free disposal of my life.

After all, it was part of the wood for me, with the trees and the eggs in the nests. I could have twisted her hair in my fists and held her under me like a devastated enemy. She would have started to cry without being able to defend herself. And then I would have walked through the woods, she would have come back to town another way. It was a feeling that perhaps came to me from my suspicious heredity. It seemed to me that this little one was, compared to my conscience as a man, an inferior humanity. There, this thing was in me like a pebble in the earth.

I felt the need to show decision. I picked up a clod of earth and threw it in front of me, saying:

- As surely as I threw this earth away, tomorrow I will go to work with them.

With the tip of her foot, she pushed the clod away and shouted sharply:

- You put her here and see, now she's over there.

I went away angrily under the trees. I felt that if only I had taken a step towards her, she would have thought: - He will make a second that will bring him back to me.

I whistled like birds in mockery of his useless rebellion; and I was already far away, I would have liked not to have left her.

- Hello ! Hello ! she cried. I heard his feet nervously hit the ground behind me. I turned my head and there she was, submissive and devious.

- Why are you angry? she says. I will go tomorrow with you to the men.

Her eyes shone ironically through her hair.

It was our last night in the wooden hut: at dawn, in the fresh sweat of the earth, with a free heart I left with her. I went to work and bread. I made there my first conscious act of man.

The morning wind twisted the smoke above the huts like light hair. As soon as we got to the table, the harsh-faced chef called one of his daughters-in-law and said:

- You will take them under your roof, like your children.

This woman then led us to the cabin and cut two large slices of bread. And then she filled a bowl with a decoction of coffee, which we passed from mouth to mouth. Then again the old man came and among themselves they called him the Father. And he says :

- There, you and she will first draw water from the pond and with this water you will soak the clay.

This man took no other care of us. He spoke little and said only the necessary words, like a king. Frilotte, with his feet in the puddle, therefore filled the tines, and I carried them towards the men responsible for kneading the earth. His patience, his goodwill now equaled my courage. She hated these people like masters, she was still too close to the free life of the woods, and yet a strange respect made her fearful: she obeyed them with humility.

She came to me under the hut at the lunch break. We broke the first bread of labor together. The woman enveloped us with defiant looks and yet did not dare to oppose the will of the Father. She tells us :

- Eat and drink.

The bread was sour and hard; the little poor like us are not difficult. But the eldest son, a head taller than me, out of play or resentment, threw a handful of sand at us, which made the mouthfuls crackle under our teeth. This one acted wickedly, for we deserved to eat the pure bread as well as he did. With the strength of a wildcat, I jumped at his throat; he rolled; I hit his face with my fists. The Father arrived at the noise of the brawl.

"Little Old Man is right," he said when he learned the reason for which we had come to blows.

He scolded the woman for giving us moldy loaf and the boy for dusting it with sand. And then she and I slept next to each other in the scorching midday. Now also the mother proved her son wrong.

Until the evening Frilotte drew water from the pond and then I rolled this water towards the area where the men were wasting. The moon rose; a light whirlwind of smoke danced at the crests of the ovens like a circle of little girls in white tunics. In the pale night the tall cones brazed; they resembled palaces on fire whose red air vents disturbed the plain. A happy weariness curled our limbs. We had taken our share of the meal together: bread and potatoes had satisfied our hunger. Now we were sitting on the threshold of the cabin and listening to the crackle of the coal. The woman called us and said:

- The boy will sleep with the boys and the girl with the girls.

Behind the closed doors, loud snores arose. Frilotte, with a proud feeling, put forward his forehead like a real little woman:

"Kiss me, Old Man," she said.

There, we were sleeping under the trees next to each other and she and I had not yet shared the kiss.

- Do what she asks of you, since she is also your wife.

Someone thus spoke of whom we did not see moving our mouths on that summer night. And I kissed her shamelessly hair.

It was the month of short nights. A light passed, the chill of dawn like a torch behind a door. Immediately the beds were tossed when I woke up. In the pale dawn, shapes rose and spread across the camp like shadows, like late parts of the night. And we too, in the dawn of gray, we were like shadows. A coolness flowed from the beech grove to this scorched and arid ground. The green scent reminded us of the solitary hut in the heart of the thicket.

With the days, regret died away: we spoke of the little wooden house without pain, as of a distant memory. The great red oaks were like parents left behind as the caravan plunged through the wide world. We can still see them for a little while and then they fade on the horizon. Frilotte now paced back and forth, awnings of fine sand in his hands; she passed this sand through a sieve and then brought it to me. I sanded with gold powder the area where the other children would dry the brick hedges before taking them to the ovens. The joy resided in our alert and precise gestures. The bread also had a more invigorating flavor since it paid us for our labor. In the evening and in the morning, one of the girls in the cabin said the prayer aloud;

When night fell, we would go and watch the ovens blazing; they dominated the bare plain. However, far away, towards the east, the lights of a city burned like lampposts. It was a very young town: perhaps there were already some unhappy people there, little poor people like us without shelter and without bread; she lined the horizon with fires. And the countryside, the arena devastated and without vegetation, always diminished a little as it advanced. It was for this city that from dawn to night, the camp worked, molding the clay into the shapes and then carrying them to the ovens. Inexhaustibly, the bricks came out of the earth, went up, stood up in red towers in simulacrum of the houses they would soon be used to build.

Everywhere the bricklayers passed, the soil emptied of its sap, a desert was born. They had been running for years; they always arrived after the harvest and then the harvest did not grow back. They were thin and parched like the earth; their eyes were consumed with fires as black as ovens. They did not know the rest of Sundays. Sometimes among themselves, with nostalgic faces, they spoke to each other about the native village. And we were, we, two little seeds of humanity, germinated from the past of cities. We had given up our free life to take our share of the sweat of working men. With the others we walked through the plain of the footsteps of a tribe. Towards evening it happened that we remained sad without a cause.

One day the chief's old wife, being at the table with the other men, passed her hand over Frilotte's forehead and said:

- Isn't that a strange thing? Our little Iule had the same look as this one.

And Iule was a girl they had once had, sleeping under a mound in the graveyard.

- There, yes, mother! you spoke the truth, cried the men. This is a strange thing.

So she got into the habit of calling him by this light and musical name; and I too end up not calling it otherwise. Iule, it was like the wind in the oaks, like the cry of a young bird, like the little water of a spring in the woods. It also sounded like the song a nanny sings near a child. She was very proud to bear a name that the master's daughter had borne. She said to me:

- Think about that. Yesterday I was Frilotte and now I am Iule. Don't you find me changed?

As they put more butter on his toast than I did, Iule scraped it with the knife and spread it on my bread. I kept calling myself the Little Old Man. Even if I changed my name, I would have remained the one who drags the burden of old humanity.

Once she began to talk to me about wood again as, in the days of our famines, she spoke to me about bread. She looked up at the trees with sharp eyes that seemed to stare at the hut. She also had another fiery and feverish voice. But I was now living tribal life; I didn't pay attention to his complaint. Showing him the cones in the plain, I say:

- They set the third oven on fire.

She didn't hear me: her soul had gone to the little green house.

However, a few days later I called Iule in vain: she did not come with the sand awnings; and then I started looking for her near the huts. She was not under the straw huts.

- She's over there in the woods, my sad heart tells me.

I went to the woods, I started running under the trees. Broken branches showed me the way she had fled. The old subtle scent, the aroma of serpolets rose from its strides and all the birds were singing. In the deep branches cried the cuckoo. Like a hiccup, like a sob passed its cry in the high green life: I had not yet heard the bird cry like this. The wood appeared to me a young eternity, a virgin mystery; I looked at him with fresh, new eyes. O what rivers of shadow flowed over my charred flesh with the fiery breath of the ovens! What divine sources of peace dripped from the slightly quivering trees! A distant voice called.

My dear Iule, here I am now near you! You rest on the old bed of leaves from our hut, you hold your feet in your hands and nothing is changed, the hut is still there as if only I had just joined the branches.

- I knew you would have come, she said, laughing frankly.

She led me to the spring, offered me the clear water in her hands and then began to straighten her hair. She had resumed her grace of a gentle wild animal, her undulating and supple life. And I, laughing like her, by madness I now kissed the trees, surrounding them with my arms. I was doing something obscure and spontaneous there that men of the ages must have done when they returned to the forest after exile from the cities. Noon fell and suddenly I thought of the tribe waiting for us near the ovens.

- Iule, I said, I came to get you. The work was in a hurry.

I spoke with decision, like a man who is aware of his duty.

- Well, she said, you will leave alone. Iule won't go with you.

- O Iule! the women baked fine French toast on the ashes.

It was because of this that she obediently followed me towards the edge. The Father with the helpers maneuvered near the table. He saw me and from a distance shouted to me:

- You wisely came back, Old Man. Now you no longer ignore what is right and what is wrong.

Iule had a different face listening to this simple word.

It rains; the windy autumn came through the woods. The doormats ran like a camp on the march; the men returned to repair the tools. A cloudy and low day slipped through the windows; You could hardly see the hands beating the chipped iron on the anvil. Now also the trees of the wood were beginning to turn red.

Then the clearings turned blue, a warmth of the sun dried up the arena; the little shadows in the pallor of dawn resumed their rhythmic gestures. A supreme ardor reigned. Iule, my dear Iule! with what zeal did your little blond clay legs run under the load of fresh bricks! You and I, over time, had become skilled workers.

The midday nap grew shorter. You no longer smoked your pipe until at night, around wood fires. So these silent men would talk to each other about the village; their faces were less gloomy, as if they were already seeing the native steeple rising behind the ovens.

One day the grandmother left for the city. Night had fallen when she returned. In the light of the lamps, fabrics were displayed; the women felt them between their fingers. There were soft clothes for the children. For the first time in our lives we felt the softness of a fabric warmly enveloping our limbs. Wool clothed our bare skins which had shivered in the breeze and burned in the sun. We dared not make a movement, for fear of offending the united weft. And I, that evening, looked with timid awkwardness at this wild girl of the woods dressed like a little Virgin of the chapels and who was spinning around, arching her waist. With a sudden cry she leapt towards the great copper shell which was heating on the stove.

- Little Old Man, is it really me? Do you still recognize me? I would never have thought myself so beautiful.

Then her thought slipped, she was there with Mama, the helpful prostitute, the poor good heart laden with sins.

- Little Old Man!… If she could see me!

Intimate and happy sensations sprang up, matched the joy of the hour. She had the awakening of the feeling of dignity, felt herself grown up, in the importance of social growth.

This was the end of the work; under cloudy low skies the light went out; the approaching stagnation of the solstice could be felt. Horse-drawn carriages were now rolling in the ravine plain, long carts which filled themselves with piles of bricks and then took the road to the city. In the red desert, among the rusty puddles, all that remained standing were the great pestles that had been opened, the jagged breach of summer cooking.

First the women left, the mothers, the grandmother, bent under the weight of the clothes: in the early morning their silhouettes were seen to diminish in the rainy air. They walked in a row, with rapid steps, taken again by the desire for the safe shelter, from the small house to the village, in the numb tranquility of winter. We stayed one day longer with the men, bringing in the straws, the tables, the molds.

- Hey ! Little Old Man, said Iule, on Sundays we go to church. I'll put on my beautiful dress. If there are shops, you will buy me earrings.

The Father removed the keys. Silence and death reigned in the old animation of the camp. And now, with the load of spades on our shoulders, taking turns to push the wheelbarrows piled up with utensils and bedding, the males of the tribe, in their turn, in the blurred light of the morning, split the plain.

We passed through villages; the white farms with red-tiled roofs, the stables scuming a hot grease, were grouped in circles around the pointed steeples. Horses pulled the plow; there were children eating thick buttered loaves on the doorsteps.

Night fell: for the poor man's money, we were lodged in a barn. The warm scent of straw enveloped us; and, with his weary little feet, Iule was beside me, his red head in my chest.

Dawn filtered through the joints of the leaves, the Father gave the signal and, once again, the roads lengthened. Towards noon, people on the thresholds began to greet us: the faces were cordial, as for an expected return.

We walked like this until nightfall. And then smoke flew, the smell of wood fires reached us from the hamlet. All the doors were open. Women with infants in their arms came forward and kissed the men.

It was there, on the edge of the moor, a hundred houses whitewashed with whitewash, among fields and orchards. Sons and fathers had come out at the time of the exodus: and now the barriers were lifted, everyone was entering the houses where little ones were born, where old people had been nailed in their coffin. Death and life had passed during their absence and they in turn arrived, thin and wandering, having won the bread of winter.

The Father pushed open a door and said:

- Here it is. You and Iule will now live in this house with our children and ourselves.

Our feet finally tasted the freshness of the tile, after the long, exhausted walk. The serge tablecloth was stretched, the pewter resounded; a thick garb smoked under the bright lamp. During the brief naps in the camp, we had not known such serious and natural pleasure.

Neighbors, tough country people, little gossips, came in and crowded near the hearth. These were talkative: they spoke of the humble splendor, the obscure destinies. The history of the hamlet, while in the desert over there the others toiled, unfolded, the harvest, the plowing, the sowing. The wheelwright had put a tiled roof over his house; the messenger's wife had had two twins; young people had exchanged promises.

What a new thing for Iule and for me! In the city as in the forest, we had lived like savages, ignoring solidarity. And now, this hamlet revealed to us the rudiments of the city according to real life, each digging and sowing for himself, but all associated with pain and interests, with a communion of misery and courage.

Iule listened, speechless, suddenly warned that there were simple souls, different from the hateful and sly market gardeners inhabiting the outskirts of the cities. Ah! we knew them well, those, lying in ambush behind the hedge with their dogs and pitchforks, hunting down the little hungry looters who were marauding a turnip at the edge of their field! The family, the social community vaguely awakened, made sense. Already at the camp, in the evening talks, we were told that there were no poor people in the hamlet. No one was rich, but everyone worked; bread was never lacking for the hunger of the little ones.

The tribe took root. The red workers of the fire were, in the fat dies of the earth, another people who had become ploughmen again. Spades dug through the courtils; the fields were filled with sudden figures dragging the harrow. The last fruits were brought in for the winter reserves; I went up to the orchard to pick the autumn purple apple. Iule cautiously gathered the harvest in the awnings. What a joy to feel and freely bite the beautiful ruddy pulps which, in the past, beyond the walled enclosures, so cruelly excited our desires! Our hands and clothes were scented with green sap. We lived there in the abundance of the goods of the earth, in the inexhaustible heart of fruiting bodies.

"Look at it, Old Man," said Iule, "once you came to the plain with me." Now we have an orchard and a house. We eat good, fresh bread. If, however, you and I had not gone to the tree, it would never have happened.

With her short forehead, she expressed there a just idea of destiny; we could not yet understand her and nevertheless she stirred something deep in us. It was like a hand that came out of a cloud and brought us to life.

The apple trees were bare: we brought in the last pickings; humble riches accumulated in the granaries. The houses resembled small roof arches which quietly awaited winter. Iule was now soaking the soup, helping the grandmother to put the bread in the oven. His hands smelled of the onion, the leek, the good herbs which perfumed the meal. The cow was also entrusted to him; she knew how to handle the needles of a knitting, and while knitting, she led the beast to graze along the road. Me, with the men, one day I went to cut the wickers, in the region of the marshes.

I knew the alternation of works which shared these humble existences. When spring came, the hamlet left to bake bricks on the outskirts of the towns. There were only old people, young mothers and the infirm in the houses. These took care of the cow, the sheep and the pig; they maintained the house and the courtyard; they watched the spelled, the rye and the potato grow in the summer sun, in the lonely expanse. We then agreed to harvest the harvest together. On the way back, the barn was full: actively, silently, the house had prepared itself to receive the tribe returned from exile. And then winter came: with flexible gestures we bent the wicker, we meshed the baskets and baskets. The ardent bricklayer of summer, the hasty worker of the last plows, became the basket maker with agile hands,

The plague beat under the awning of the barns. I carried the grain to the mill; I pushed a full wheelbarrow in front of me. I had good times among the flour-makers with the white masks, in the pale house where the flour was snowing. The roar of the wings turning on their axes reminded me gently of the dull thunder of the bridges above my sleeps huddled in the ribs of the iron.

The poor boy is an observer: he grasps the analogies. His head works like the mill crushes the fatty pulp of the grain. With the wind of chance, she too, in the immense daily adventure of life, makes her flour from everything that passes through her hopper. I watched the slow gesture of the flour makers under the high powdered joists pouring the sack of grain into the conduits, stopping or setting the cleat in motion. They were silent and patient, like all those who help themselves by the forces of nature. When the wind stopped blowing, the mill was idle; and whistling melancholy tunes softly, they waited for the wind to pick up. I whistled like them.

My life shot up. I felt that I too, by bringing the ground grain home, was doing something useful. The mill grinds the wheat and then, in the hollow of the corn, fists actively knead the flour. I was the intermediary between the maie and the mill. When the bread finally rose, I was conscious of having taken my share of the work. It was a warmth of joy and pride, like doing good and deserving of life. Now that the reflection has come to me, I admire what helping forces, what reserves of courage and wisdom lie at the bottom of the most destitute being. It was only a little while ago that I had ceased to be a little vagabond, mingled with the lamentable wrecks that the muddy river of cities carries; and already, by the power of example, at the approaches of a simple and cordial humanity, I felt within me the movements of a consciousness. However, there, tortured by hunger, it could have happened to me one day to steal a loaf of bread from the baker's counter. The whole social apparatus would have shaken to lead me to the judge. He would have easily established that I was a precocious criminal because, in a hypocritical and cowardly society, hunger, even more than the theft of bread, is an attack on public morals. I who was a child given birth in the shade of a porch and to whom no one had learned to work, I who had grown to life like weeds from the edge of the ditches, I would have become, in the corrosive dormitories of a house of correction, a perverted being, with cautious eyes, a heart fermented with hatred and revolt. One day it could have happened to me to steal a loaf of bread from the baker's counter. The whole social apparatus would have shaken to lead me to the judge. He would have easily established that I was a precocious criminal because, in a hypocritical and cowardly society, hunger, even more than the theft of a loaf of bread, is an attack on public morals. I who was a child given birth in the shade of a porch and to whom no one had learned to work, I who had grown to life like weeds from the edge of the ditches, I would have become, in the corrosive dormitories of a house of correction, a perverted being, with cautious eyes, a heart fermented with hatred and revolt. One day it could have happened to me to steal a loaf of bread from the baker's counter. The whole social apparatus would have shaken to lead me to the judge. He would have easily established that I was a precocious criminal because, in a hypocritical and cowardly society, hunger, even more than the theft of bread, is an attack on public morals. I who was a child given birth in the shade of a porch and to whom no one had learned to work, I who had grown to life like weeds from the edge of the ditches, I would have become, in the corrosive dormitories of a house of correction, a perverted being, with cautious eyes, a heart fermented with hatred and revolt. in a hypocritical and cowardly society, hunger, even more than the theft of bread, is an attack on public morals. I who was a child given birth in the shade of a porch and to whom no one had learned to work, I who had grown to life like weeds from the edge of the ditches, I would have become, in the corrosive dormitories of a house of correction, a perverted being, with cautious eyes, a heart fermented with hatred and revolt. in a hypocritical and cowardly society, hunger, even more than the theft of bread, is an attack on public morals. I who was a child given birth in the shade of a porch and to whom no one had learned to work, I who had grown to life like weeds from the edge of the ditches, I would have become, in the corrosive dormitories of a house of correction, a perverted being, with cautious eyes, a heart fermented with hatred and revolt.

The first snow flaked: the orchards, the roofs of butter and tiles sank into a white silence. Intimacy then withdrew to the heart of the houses, a quiet life of silence and waiting near the domestic animals. The clock, in the warmth of the hearths, punctuated the active hours, the rhythm of the hands plaiting the wicker, the soft and silent relaxation of the vigil over the filth fire. The whole hamlet, behind the windows, was shaping awnings, baskets to drain the cheese and delicate baskets. We could hear the heavy ruminating of the cows at the back of the stables, the splashing of the pigs in the trough; and the roads were empty, there was no other noise. All ties seemed severed with the outside world. However in the morning a lapping of children's hooves trailed, girls and boys in small bands, blue nose and hands in mittens. It was the shoemaker Jean's class. The hooves meandered for a little while along the hedges and then struck the threshold of a low door. We went with the others. In a room with scrambled windows, an old man, with glasses on his nose, pricked the awl and pulled the thread with his big pitch black hands.

Three benches lined up near the cast iron stove. There were antique pictures and books on the wall in the chest: they helped the old man to meditate on things in the universe. For almost sixty years that he had been in the hamlet, his life had been spent loving others and reseeding the country, in this humble corner of the world. He had had no other ambition, letting the little children come to him, teaching them what with great brain effort, without the help of any master, he himself had learned in his images and in his books. My God ! his books ! Old almanacs, Mathieu Laensbergs from the year fifteen with jagged and shriveled leaves, as if nibbled by mice, stained by the wet nudge with which he spun them, yellowed and mottled on a par with the skin of his hands ! He also had some fragments of the Gospels.

"Christ passed by this morning," said John gravely. He came in here, he sat here, he said beautiful things to me which I will tell you in turn.

Not everyone believed him, but I looked at the chair he was pointing at. I was sure it had happened as he said, and Christ had set in the chair. It seemed to me that he must look like him.

With the trembling of his big glasses on his nose stinged with black holes, he would start from there to explain to us that it is necessary to love others as oneself, to share with the poor his misery and not to harm animals.

I think with emotion of the good man Jean. He comes back to life from the past of my life as a humble village saint. If I succeeded later in disentangling good from evil, I, the little vagabond with a dark soul, it is to him, to the great light which fell from his open hands that I owe it. However hardly it passed in my life and it never went away.

Sitting among us, his corded hands running along the lines, he read us the texts, explained the old symbols to us. It was the astrologer with the pointed hat, the dress studded with moons and stars; they were the months and the seasons, the solstices, the equinoxes; they were fables, proverbs and sentences. I knew the Golden Days of the calendar; the great Beatified appeared to me to be ancestors, grandfathers haloed and glorified for having done their duty on earth.

He also taught us to spell and write. In thick chalk writing he traced letters on the chest which we then had to recopy until both sides of our slates were filled with them. The key creaked, mishandled by the stiff fingers; while we were applying ourselves to our jambs, he went off for a little while to beat a pan end at his table. Other times, by emptying a bag of chestnuts onto the tile, he would teach us arithmetic. Two and two is four and four is eight, and four times eight ... Who would have ever said, little Iule, that one day you too could count to a hundred?

When the old man said: "Take a good look at me. It is I who am God and I push the earth like this and the moon like that, "I truly believed that God was before me and was revealing the great mystery to me.

The little school ended at noon. Then, as in the morning, the hooves began to beat again along the hedges. Sometimes a brawl arose. The big ones were rushing on the little ones. Iule and I were banging our fists: we dreaded it. When we returned, the potato was smoking on the table. There was the father and three of his sons there, seated around the hearth on low stools, with the tools and fresh wickers. They only stopped moving their hands to eat and then worked until the evening. Iule had taken a liking to this work; I was less skilled at it than she was. The wickers under his precise fingers unrolled like slender snakes. She twisted them, meshed them into delicate corbels. In the silent winter of the house, the clock beat with a slow pulse, the lamp was lit,

This monotonous life gently numbed us. The other winter I had frozen under the bridges, Iule one night had almost never woken up again: it was Mama who had brought her back to life by laying her near her in her warmth of love. What had become of her in her poor life of misery and abjection? Ah yes ! what had become of poor Mama with her colorful old rags, with the shawl with holes under which, like an image of gallant death, she strutted in the impure evening of the streets, whispering cuddly invites to passers-by? She was already coughing at this time with such a dreadful rattle of alcohol and consumption!

Yes, it was a happy time. The house, the ancient family tradition, must be deeply embedded in the heart of the races to revive the instinct for sociability so quickly. Like free wild beasts, we had lived, on the borders of humanity, the adventure of days. And our fibers were already recovering from the lively heat of contact.

An obscure filiality palpitated, softened me to the common life near the ancestor and the grandmother. Iule also seemed changed. She no longer swore by the holy names. Words, reminders of filthy things faded away. Its cunning and sly funds of nature were, as it were, limited to the probity of this loyal and gentle people.

Yes, I was fooled like everyone else by his little comedy of dissimulation. I didn't know why sometimes she stuck her tongue out behind the backs of the people who were there and then strangely looked at me laughing. When I began to see clearly in her, it seemed to me that she instinctively had two souls, her Sunday soul that she spent with her beautiful dress, a frank and amused soul with which she looked at herself in the mirror and went to hear mass. in the village a league from the hamlet, and then the other, clandestine and stubborn, his little soul of misery and vice over there in the city.

One day the trees sprouted and the time for baskets was over. There came from the birds; the green sap rose. The land was prepared for the sowing. All the houses were empty and Iule began to tell me about the forest again. I listened to him absent-mindedly at first. My life was more with these men who bowed in the pink countryside. The small class had ended with snow and winter. The clogs no longer knocked on the door of the gentle ingenuous master: by the green paths they left for another school far away where a real master taught according to the principles. On the last day Jean gravely took one of his ancient almanacs and put it in my hands, saying:

- You are not like the others. I read things in your eyes. If one day you are unhappy or if you need advice, open the book, you will find the right lesson there.

It was for me like a legacy of life, like a religious gift; the book fluttered near my flesh under my shirt.

One morning with an overcast sky, the doors banged: it was Easter Monday. The men, laden with shovels and bags, left as they had returned. Every year, on the same day, rain or sun, we emigrated with the herds in heaps in wheelbarrows. The Father went ahead and the sons followed. The women then arrived, found the camp set up. A few old people remained alone in the houses for sowing and the cradles. We passed through the villages; on the thresholds, as at the time of the return, children were eating buttered bread; and the hedges were green. I had a knife, good shoes, a stick in my hand. I felt like a man and my whole life ahead of me.

Iule, in the evening, had strange eyes.

- Think then, Old Man, she said, if the little house was still there?

My heart pounded strongly; all the green wood passed. O Iule! the little hut under the young shoots of leaves! The wind like the breath of a sleeping mouth! The rain like light footsteps approaching! I was no longer with the men. She laughed and whispered into my neck:

- The house thinks of us as we think of it, Old Man.

She didn't say anything else, and I, seeing her cunning eyes, trembled as if she had already taken me by the hand and was leading me towards the hut. If I had taken a step into the woods, maybe I would never have come back. I shook my head.

- You see, Iule, there were rains and snows.

And then I was in front of her, my mouth empty of words. I no longer dared to follow my thought through.

Immediately life in the camp resumed, it seemed to have been interrupted only the day before. The mats on the men's backs ran brandished, standing like moving tents. The wood fires fumed under the pot. With bare heels, Iule and I paced the area where a poor grass thin as the hair of a scabby animal in places had grown back. Now the team with its huts was advancing to virgin lands. The ancient devastation of the desert remained behind us. Fields that were still green were smashed up, thick with the sap of recent crops. The Father himself with the masters of the fund had set the limits. It was almost thirty years since a morning he had come for the first time and each year the countryside receded, cut through by the breaches, eaten up by the baking of the ovens while, on the other hand, in the jagged horizon,

The forest, with all its light and green mass, was now there, in the young April rains. Iule sometimes prowled around me, looking at me with sly eyes. When evening fell, she disappeared into the woods. Once I watched for her. The small shadow, in the night of the trees, ardently burrowed under the mosses, at the base of an oak. My breath gasped: she saw me near her and immediately, with a cry of anger, she let herself fall, flattened herself stiffly on the hole she was digging. I was very gentle and clever. She reassured herself; she laughed with hidden and bold eyes:

- Little Old Man, won't you tell anyone?

- No.

- Well, I found something and hid it there. See!

She scratched in the hole and pulled out a small box with an earring in it.

- Iule, you're lying! I cried. You stole this buckle from the old woman.

I stepped on her and tried to tear the box away from her; but she held it in her clenched hand, her fingernails scratching my face.

- Give it to me, give it to me! I still cried.

We struggled. With a bound she escaped and, at a short distance, with wicked joy, she challenged me and silently said:

- She's mine ! I stole it! I stole it! She's mine !

I began to whistle quietly between my teeth, and then, after a little while, I said to him:

- See now: this woman loved you like a girl and you stole her.

She cried once more, ringing the gold of the pendant:

- She's mine. I'll make a little hole in my ear, I'll put it through the hole. If anyone says this thing is not mine, they lied about it.

I answered him gently:

- There is only one loop and you have two ears. How will you manage to put a piece of it together?

- Oh ! she said, I hadn't thought about what you're saying yet. The buckle was in the drawer there: there was only one and I took it. I wouldn't have taken them both.

- If I were you, Iule, I would bring it back to the old woman, since you just as well have two ears and you have only one ring. I would say to him: I took this buckle from the trunk and now I'm giving it to you. She'll get mad and then she'll forget you went to the safe. I assure you, that's what is best.

- Yes, she cried happily, that's what is best.

I took a step, I thought she would give me back the loop. But she backed up behind a tree and laughed.

- After all, isn't she mine, since I have her? In the trunk it belonged to no one and now I hold it in my hands. Why would one have something the other doesn't have?

There, this little girl, in her dull brain, was telling a terrifying truth. If one has a piece of bread that is denied to the hunger of another, it is he who is the thief. Everything should be shared between men, and who has two earrings may well give one to someone who does not. However I say to Iule:

- Think about this: the old woman paid the buckle with her money, and if she asked you the price she gave, you could not return it to her.

- Well, she said, go and put it back in the safe yourself. When she opens it, she will see the buckle and she will not think of anything else.

His eyelids fluttered; she had a small, dry pain that clenched her mouth.

- I had kept it hidden on my skin for a while. She shone so sweetly in the sun! If you had seen her hanging from my ear, you would have thought you saw another girl. Oh ! I hate her, that old woman! Why did she say sweet words to me?

I opened her fingers, she finally let go of the loop and then I, with the cry of force and cunning, I ran towards the camp.

- She's mine, Iule! If you say I stole it, I'll strangle you.

The Mother was in the cabin with the men: it was the end of a day's work. No one noticed that I was holding something in my hands. I had come with the firm intention of returning the buckle to the old woman, and now I was there, mouth closed, feeling in my turn a singular joy in holding this little treasure between my fingers. I thought: since she doesn't know anything, it might as well keep this to myself. At the end of the room was the lean-to where the two old people slept; I knew the safe was near the door. The men now, with heavy sleep gestures, made their way to the beds. I made my way to the door. I told myself that once in the lean-to, I would open the trunk very quickly and throw the buckle in it. But the Mother said to me:

- Where are you going over there, Old Man?

I could have told her that I had to go into the lean-to for something that did not concern her or else simply put the buckle back to her by saying: "There, Iule took it and I put it back in the trunk." But suddenly I thought that if I said it that way, there would be great anger in the house against Iule. I was there in front of the door, my eyes down, not knowing what story to imagine. And then once again I felt the strange charm of gold on my fingers. My teeth clenched; I couldn't have made a sound out of it. It will be tomorrow, I thought, when no one is in the house anymore. At this moment Iule returned; I heard the beating of her little bare feet near me. With a breath on my neck, she asked me:

- Did you really throw it at the bottom of the trunk?

And I tell him:

- I did it.

However, I still held the loop in my hands.

The next day I spent the day soaking the clays. Iule never worked far from me: she came and went with the water from the tine. Grudge was brewing in his sidelong eye. Several times she asked me if it was really true that I had put the buckle back in the trunk. I just shook my head without saying yes or no. There was not the slightest bit of honesty in all of this; I no longer had the same feeling of good conscience as the day before. She, at least, had yielded to instinct, to the natural pleasure of stealing a jewel to adorn it. The hands of the poor are sprawling; but I, by delaying restoring the gold buckle, seemed to give myself time to use the movements of my integrity.

Iule, during the midday rest, came to lie down beside me. She held her feet in her hands, which in her was a sign of reflection, and she looked at me frankly.

- You see, Old Man, she said, if you hadn't done it, this loop would now be yours. I would never have asked for it again.

- Well, there you go, I replied. Yesterday, the Mother prevented me from going to the chest. I hid it between the boards.

She said to me quietly:

- You didn't hide it between the planks. The buckle is in your pocket. If you believe me, now that you've gotten used to it, you'll keep it for both of us.

That was the terrible thing, I was starting to get used to, as she said, the idea of always having the light weight of that gold close to my living flesh. I wouldn't have had the same courage if I had had to go to the safe at the moment. It's not a day's business, I thought, since the old woman didn't notice a thing either.

So she slipped her arm under my neck; and she asked me nothing, she caressed me with affectionate affection.

"I'm sick of the woods," she said. Feel how my hands are burning. Why did we come to these men? There we would have lived together without being accountable to anyone. You and I would have worked freely for us. Little old man, I assure you, it would have been better for both of them.

Her voice whispered softly near my ear; and now, leaning on my elbow, I was looking at the green line of the forest in the clear sky. I held my teeth clenched, as if to stop my heart from coming out. But she always followed her idea and below she said:

- We would leave in the evening when the men are in the house. No one would know where we went and each of us in turn would carry this thing for a little while. Think about it: there would never be anyone to claim it from us.

A heat rose in my life. I would have liked to cry, with my heart swelling like a bean in my hands. There were already such strong bonds between me and this family of chance! And yet the fragrant forest also called me. Iule's voice in my ear was like the brushing of the wind from under the trees. I turned around so as not to see the peaks anymore and in this movement I suddenly felt that she was trying to put her hand in my pocket. She saw herself surprised and immediately began to cry out horrible curses; all the dregs of the city rose; and now she felt forever defeated, delivered to me.

The Father, from the threshold of the house, clapped his hands; the men one after the other got up to resume work and until evening Iule, with his dark passion, remained silent. Me, at times I felt the loop at the bottom of my pocket. I no longer had the same joy, understanding that it would be perpetually a subject of irritation and resentment between us. I thought: What are you going to become with this that you will always have to hide? If you don't return it, we will all the same suspect at the end that it was Iule or you who stole it. The temptation of the wood returned, persisted, impunity after the bad deed, the sure mystery of the hiding places where no one would go to discover us. Night fell and she kindly came to me. She tells me :

- Whether you keep it or give it back, I don't care now. Do as you like. I will never tell you about it again.

- Iule! Iule! I cried, why did you take it? All the evil came from there. Now we just have to hide in the woods. We could no longer live with these people.

Iule laughed softly, followed his idea. She tells me :

- Once we're in the woods, we won't mind what they think of us.

I could not have explained how it happened that suddenly I thought I felt the almanac beating in my chest.

I always carried it with me, opening it sometimes and, one finger on the letters, trying to get to the end of the lines. He seemed to be saying to me: Do it! Do it ! But the Father called us; the other men were already asleep.

- Tomorrow, little Iule! Tomorrow…

She lay down on the bale of straw: the door was closed; and over the roar of the bedroom, her voice rose softly.

- Good evening, Old Man… Tomorrow, tomorrow…

At dawn the house emptied and I, with careful steps, listening to the voices in the distance in the camp, I went to the safe. It was locked, the Mother had removed the key; and the curl between my fingers, I was now looking at the chest with a great pang of heart. Iule, coming on my heels, bravely said to me:

- Since that is as well, put her on the bed. We have nothing more to hide now. She will find her there when she comes home and she will understand why we left.

I threw the buckle on the bed. Immediately our feet ran; the forest opened up: we did not stop running until we failed to breathe.

We rolled over to the warm earth bed and Iule was hiding something behind her. We were there for a while as if passed out to life, with the panting of our chests. No rumor arose from the camp; silence, the great cool peace of the foliage enveloped us. I was happy, I didn't have a grudge against Iule. She had done the wrong: I had not separated from her in the consequences of the wrong action: I had taken my share of the fault fraternally. If she had had to be taken to prison, I would have liked to be taken there with her. These were very subtle thoughts for a young boy. And yet it was deep in me, in the unexpressed part of my life, like an awakening of my still obscure intimate beauty.

O my dear Iule, I had borne your fault as a heavy penalty and now, having accepted to be separated from other men because of her, I felt above me a very sweet thing, confusedly rising from the bottom of my life, and which mingled with the goodness of nature. I then took your hands in mine; I looked you in the eye and couldn't tell you anything. I had never felt closer to you than through the shared fault which so intimately confused our two destinies. You didn't speak to me either, but a clarity passed in your eyes, your chest shook, and now perhaps you realized that I had given you my life.

The flies vibrated reddish; the golden shower of noon filtered under the leaves; and the old hunger of the poor began again. Iule disappeared for a while behind the trees and then I saw her come back, loaded with an old bag. I understood that was what she had kept hidden behind her.

Now, without saying anything, with an ant's nervous activity, she opened the bag and took out of it bread, prunes, nuts, dried apple wedges, a bottle, a chipped plate. With every object she spread out in front of me, she looked at me, laughing with her happy little wow. She also took the shoes and clothes that she and I wore there on Sunday. Ah! those we had deserved by our work the other summer; they had been the wages of the sorrow taken in common. My God ! it was a really funny thing that she had thought of all this! We had a plate as if to eat again the appetizing garbure the old woman was making.

I too cried out with pleasure. However, I could not understand how she had obtained the prunes and apple quarters: since the end of winter the supply had been exhausted. All her wonderful concealment was revealed: she told me that in anticipation of our return to the forest, she had spared them on her meals, hiding them as they went in the old bag.

She thus rose very high above the other girls, those who ran barefoot in the stream in the city, and also those who, with wise little faces, went to listen to mass in the village. She was before my eyes like an Iule that I did not yet know. O Iule! me there I had forgotten the happy life under the trees, happy to be well fed; but you, you had kept your wild energies; you were always the free little beast that yearned for the hairy bosom of the forest.

With my head higher and my knife in my pocket, I felt ashamed to feel inferior to this little girl who had resolutely arranged in her head the plan of our escape. She took eight prunes, kept only two for herself; and then she broke the bread and gave me most of it. There she was doing what an elder sister would have done. We were rich and free; we didn't think apples and prunes would ever end. We had life ahead of us.

A chill rose: it was the hour when the gold of the last rays over there enveloped the camp; our long shadows the day before had run over the clay desert, in the haste of the final labor. I felt nothing but contempt for these men who had been my family. The wild madness of the wood intoxicated me. If one of them had come to take us back, I would have pulled my knife. After all, we were the masters of our skins. The stolen property had been returned: we no longer owed anyone anything.

- Little old man ! she said as the first time she came with me under the trees, I can't take it anymore. Sit there, I'll lay my head on your shoulder.

It had been so long since we had slept like this. Iule, with her life against my life, became again the confident little child who had left the city behind to follow me. We were no more than one and the same destiny in the soft clear night in the woods, as if no man had yet said to us: "You are a boy and you are a girl." I held his heavy head in my arm.

We awoke with a blue sky in our eyes, and as the day before she took the bread out of the bag, she divided it into two parts; and the biggest was for me. And then, hand in hand, we set off to explore the hut. But the branches had tangled on our old paths; the strides of our footsteps had disappeared, lost under the tall green shoots. When noon fell, Iule as in the morning gave me six prunes and she took two for herself. We kept listening to the buzzing of the flies around us. Sometimes she caught one in flight and gently tore off its wings. Once again the trees began to throb again in the evening; I had his fresh life in my chest.

- Will we ever find the little green house? she said.

And she fell asleep. But the next day, having walked in front of us, a cry came to us at the same time. The hut !

The ash sprigs that I had intertwined with the oak branches now stirred with a life of little leaves around the dead wood. Little primitive house, you had continued to live there as a part of us, leaving us with the mild pain of something that was like our torn fibers, clinging to another lost life. It had been made from one of our thoughts and it had grown up on its own; she had, in the mystery of the deep woods, flowered with young spring. What an incredible surprise! We walked around the humble shelter, Iule uttering his little animal cries, I silent and serious, like the Little Old Man whose name I bore.

I was proud and amazed to have built it. Yes, I was there, in front of the hut, like a human creature who, after a long absence, sees his house again. It only takes a little goodwill for man to secure a home, and then nature works to keep it for him. Mosses fluffed the shelter, the leaves were shaded by a mobile life; only the roof, under the weight of the snow, had sagged.

My heart slowly rose, stirred by deep things I could not have said. Perhaps it was the silent thanksgiving for the beauty of life and all the eternity of life that there is in a branch which turns green with each spring. We do not know what is going on in the depths of a soul which has learned nothing and which lives on its own powers. And Iule too could not have said for what cause all of a sudden, after looking at me with her hand in mine, she withdrew it and began to sob, hiding from me to cry between her fingers.

A nearby oak tree had a large crack: it became our loft of plenty. As a wise housewife, she put our reserves of apples and prunes there; and we had some bread left. She said to me quietly:

- Once again, it's nest time. When we have eaten all the bread, you will go up to the trees and take the eggs.

She spoke there like a child who has confidence in life.

I passed my knife back over a stone and, having gained the heart of the woods, came back with large branches. I assembled them and tied them with flexible twigs. They covered the hut with a light and solid vault. As I was finishing this work, Iule came to me and, resting his hand on my arm, said softly:

- Do you hear the bird singing over there?

His voice sounded different from that of men. I didn't know which bird she was talking to me about. But, having come out of the hut, in my turn I listened and then very far away I heard the cuckoo. He sang three times and then again, after a while, he began to sing again. He seemed to welcome us as on the first day. This one, among the other birds, was the benevolent and lonely little soul of the forest. Iule and I, listening to him sing, we no longer spoke; it was as if something had stirred in us that was still unknown to us. And then he fell silent and then we started shouting cuckoo! with madness.

My God ! That night, under the green shelter! That night when for the first time, with the warmth of her innocent life against mine, I had the anguish of knowing that she was different from me! An unknown fire consumed me. I was burning and my limbs were frozen; I felt awfully sad as if something had happened that was going to change us for each other. My hand timidly tried the outline of her chest. My fingers had caresses that would have wanted to hurt him tenderly. I was like someone who has entered a garden full of golden fruits and who, with these beautiful fruits in his hand, is devoured with a thirst that he cannot quench. I would have fled in fear if she hadn't suddenly woken up and looked at me in the night. No, I had not yet felt such bitter pain. Dawn began to filter through the branches of the roof and only then did I fall asleep. When I opened my eyes, Iule was leaning over me smoothing my hair.

- You screamed last night, she said. I was still sleeping and your screams woke me up. I thought you were upset: you didn't answer me. So gently I took your head against me.

- There, yes, I dreamed, Iule.

- Oh ! she said, I too had a dream. I was near you and you were biting me with your mouth. It was really good. You had eyes like I've never seen you before. Your hands would not let go: I was crying and I was happy.

Weeping, I started to cry Iule! Iule! and then I couldn't think of anything more to say to him. All my pain had returned and yet I was happy that she had suffered because of me. It was a deep and dark thing in the depths of my life as if, in the same minute, we had bled deliciously from such a brotherly wound. And tenderly Iule, with whispering words, consoled me.

- What's wrong with you, Old Man? I haven't done anything to you though. But if you're sad about this other thing, you'd be wrong, I assure you. It was sweet like when Mama gave me too much to drink. She was always drinking something sweet whose name I forgot. On the days when there were men, she drank a whole bottle; and yet there were always three or four glasses for me. So everything was turning and I was happy. Believe me, I would like to go to sleep right away to feel this again.

But there ! I had put my hands on his flesh like a thief. I was left with great confusion. I went into the woods, I felt the need to be some time alone with myself. So I walked in front of me whistling. I told him: "I will go up to the trees if there are nests." But now I was no longer thinking of the nests. I let myself fall, my heart was beating in my hands and I didn't know what ailment I was suffering from; I only knew that Iule was a woman like this Mama who went into her miserable garret with men. I never dreamed that I would ever hate her because of it. O Iule! you were no longer the wild little sister who ran with a shred of skirt on her thighs and whose breast had not yet risen. It was a strange mixture of fear and aversion that you inspired in me. And there I was screaming and cursing, rolling on the moss with a bowel warmth. If you had come then, I would have taken you by the hair, I would have dragged you to the ground. Your tears would have made me happy.

And then suddenly I stopped hating her; all I wanted to do was find myself with her. My fibers relaxed; the dry fury softens. With a dash I ran, I split the green branches and from afar, with the good brotherhood returned, I called him.

- Iule! Iule!

The hut was empty. My call was lost in the high branches and I was no longer angry. I was sad, with great cowardly grief, as if half of my life was no longer there. The absence continued. I dreaded a ruse, the mobility of his stealthy, clandestine heart. I think if she hadn't come back, I would have broken my head against a tree trunk. I stayed a long time with strained ears, listening to the sounds of the woods. The wind had risen, a broad and sonorous wave which crumpled the summits and made the continuous sound of a river: there was a river crossing the city. She was suddenly near me in that green swell, without my having heard her coming, and with low eyes she was laughing. Me neither, I dared to look at her frankly.

- Did you find any nests? she says.

- There were no nests where I passed.

She clapped her hands happily.

- Oh ! Little Old Man, don't say that. The wood is full of nests. But there you are, you lay down under a tree.

- Well yes. It was hot, I replied. You too, Iule, have foam in your hair.

She was looking over her shoulder at the trees, far away.

- If you think that I also slept, she said, it is not true. Ah! Little old man !

She sighed: she wanted to tell me something and she was silent. Maybe she didn't know herself what she wanted to tell me. And now she was gently wringing her hands together, weary of boredom.

- I assure you, she said, I don't know what you have against me. You are not the same boy you used to be.

My heart rose; however, I could find nothing to say to him. She took her hair in her hands, unfurled it and laughed through it, saying in mockery:

- You cry at night; and by day you keep your teeth clenched.

Once again I would have beaten her, I couldn't say why.

That evening she only gave me three prunes; and we started to store apples. We had eaten the last piece of bread in the morning. Neither of us had any concerns for the future. Something had happened that tormented us more than hunger. The shadow spread, the night stirred in the leaves. The trees swayed like ships in the harbor. She took my hand and said:

- Come into the house. The wind scares me. I won't hear it again when you take my head in your arms.

She had cut some fresh ferns; their thickness softly covered the ground; and now, nestled in my chest, she was laughing.

- Oh ! how good the wind is! The whole earth is shaking and I am no longer afraid.

Her knees to her chin, holding her hands crossed between her small breasts, almost immediately she fell asleep from her childish sleep. But I, in the terrible shock of the gusts, stayed awake for a long time. Sudden shocks beat the light roof. A big branch cracked, smashed small trees near us. The whole forest roared like a millstone. With the warm throbbing of this little life of Iule in my shoulder, I felt a great softness. The sound of the wind, the drowsy smell of ferns at the end put me to sleep. And then in the morning the rain fell. We awoke to the tinkling of water streaming from the tall foliage. The wood was strewn with debris.

Days passed: time ceased to exist. I climbed the trees; I stole nests. Iule liked to see the agony of little beasts under his fingers; There was a background of quiet cruelty in his nature, and I hadn't yet learned to respect life either.

It was the season of love: he flew little gray feathers in the air and the mothers themselves with their cries pointed out to us the place of the broods. She learned to climb branches; sometimes she brought me fresh wild-tasting eggs. We roasted the little ones over wood fires that I lit by beating the flint. The water from the spring near the pond then quenched our thirst. Small industries came to us: I cut records with a knife; they served us as plates. At the tip of the blade, I had carved animal shapes on the gnarled holly, which I brandished like a scepter. I had also dug a boxwood root: it took the drawing of a pipe. I smoked dry chestnut leaves there. Iule for her part braided mats which covered the roof and stopped the rain.

Sometimes we would walk for days on end, pushing in front of us at random and breaking branches in the thickets to find our way back. When evening fell, Iule spread a layer of ferns and then in the morning we started walking again: we seemed to be discovering the world. New essences were revealed to us; trees dotted with unknown fruits with delicious green juice. We let the pink juice of the first strawberries melt slowly on the tongue. With each find, she had her cry. Wow ! Wow ! We were the young kings of the silve; it seemed to us that we would never have finished going around it. So we went, carrying our shoes wisely on our backs to spare the soles. On the way back, the little green house living in the sun its quivering life of clear leaves gave us joy. Yes, it was a great happiness for two scraps of humanity like us, to have no masters and to live freely in the heart of nature.

One day, returning from my nest hunt, I looked in vain for Iule. The heavy noon was burning. I thought she had taken the cool path to the pond. And, as I in my turn approached, I saw him bathing behind the leaves. In the past, with water up to our knees, we had entered this great green puddle: I had not yet felt the fear of his body. And now she was there in her nakedness, like a little Eve. Her light flesh had the beauty of a flower of life in the innocent landscape. She drew the water in the hollow of her hands and let it run between the points of her throat; or else she would dive under the lenses which fluffed the pool, and remain lost for a while in the cold chill of the bath.

In the ardent silence, the foliage stirred: she raised her head, uttered a cry, and I had already fled. With the mystery of his life in my eyes, I plunged into the woods. If she had called me, I would not have come back: I was sick with a very gentle and fierce pain, as if I myself had suddenly been naked in front of her. I would have liked to have lived alone for a long time in the depths of the shadows, still watching the small spot of light that it made in the water move. I neither loved nor hated her; but now I knew that something in me was still unknown to me, a terrible and delicious thing that demanded to live the rest of my life. The marriageable and original being shuddered to desire himself before desiring the complementary substance. I rolled on the ground, I bit the ground; at the pain of the wound, I felt myself becoming a man. And as I was there, tearing myself apart with my hands, suddenly the old almanac, the good teacher's lesson rolled away. I always carried it with me, like a little relic, like a talisman; it was beating close to my heart; I had never spent a day without spelling out his naive fables. O Monsieur Jean! Monsieur Jean!

There was a story above all, an old man living in a desert, among stones and evil beasts. He had come to these dreaded places in the troubled blood age. He had killed, he had stolen, he had done evil in every way. The late good conscience had finally appeared and then the desert had changed into a garden of abundance and joy. The stones, watered with his repentant tears, had blossomed: the tigers and the lions were innocent flocks; and because he himself had returned to goodness, all things around him became good in his image. I had read it a hundred times, this lovely tale, and it always seemed new to me, with a parabolic and universal meaning. A poor little contemplative hears the song of the birds and he grasps the secret reports of things: he is closer to nature and to himself. The gentle master told me:

- Don't stop thinking about this story of the wicked man in the desert. Think about it especially when you are about to fail in your consciousness. You will see that it applies to all men and it only takes good will to change pebbles into wheat and the worst animals into gentle sheep. A little book like this contains all human knowledge: but the best knowledge is still that which comes to us to look deep inside.

Yes, a simple hamlet shoemaker, with his glasses on his nose, so the true word tells me. And now, listening to him in my life, I knew that I too was a man living in the desert among wild beasts.

That night and the nights that followed, I took her head in my arms, as she liked to fall asleep; and then slowly, when sleep came, I would lay her down on the ferns and go to sleep in the wood. There was a bitter pleasure there for me as if, in doing this, I was a man who already holds in the palm of his hand his powers of will. If the old man in the desert had not had them, he would not have turned the tigers into sheep. But on the tenth night, thunder rumbled, horror was over the forest and Iule said to me:

- See, if now I was killed what would become of you?

She could just as well have said the opposite and then she would have thought only of her own life; but with her tender heart she took death for herself and saw me forever unhappy. It was such a sweet thing to hear him speak to me like that. Yes, I thought, better as she said. What would become of me in the forest on my own? But immediately I cried:

- Don't say that, little Iule. See, I put myself on top of you, I hide you with my body. I assure you, it is I who will die first.

She fell asleep and I tenderly watched over this life she had abandoned to me in thought. She was like a fearful little child in my hands and I had forgotten that she had been naked in front of my eyes. In the morning all the birds sang.

Now, when the wind picked up, we climbed the trees, I climbed the tallest branches. We liked to sway to the rolling summits: it left us the feeling of a life of squirrels and birds mingled with forces and space. The turmoil beneath us swirled in green eddies. Clinging tightly to the creaking of the branches, we plunged into the void, from the height of a sky, and then again we flew, we were carried to the currents. A delicious horror gripped our nerves. She uttered her wild wow and I laughed, in a madness of heroism. The wind shook us, threw us towards each other. Sometimes I watched for the passage of the gust, I suddenly let go, I threw my hands forward in the enormous furious wave: it carried me to Iule. And this storm music,

It occurred to us to spend our nights there. An ancient beech, of tormented sap, bifurcated halfway up, as if split with an ax. A nearby oak helped us to hoist us up to the fork. I pulled her by the wrists and with a small jerk of the kidneys in turn she was removed. The vast undulating night of the forest made its murmur on us: we fell asleep in starlight, rocked by light breezes, as on a raft. What deep rise of the races gave us a taste for this winged life where at the same time we tasted the joy of adventure and security in peril? The primary substance without our knowledge stirred in our blood returned to the savagery of the man of the woods.

Our provisions had long been exhausted: we were constantly forced to vary our plans. There were no more eggs in the nests: the chicks had taken flight. To appease our hunger, sometimes, after endless watchings at the edge of a clearing, I would kill a rabbit, with a stone surely thrown. We had to walk for hours before reaching the strawberry and blueberry region. However, we were much happier than with the men. They had been helpful and kind to us; they had taught me the virtue of honestly earned bread; we had known under their roof a truce to the harsh existence. And now, the mad sap of nature had been stronger.

Once I spoke to Iule about our old life in the camp: she began to bite her nails and then bitterly regretted the gold buckle. She swore like a pagan, like this Mama in town when men had paid her badly. Little old man ! I thought, better keep your ideas to yourself from now on. It is not good to tell girls everything. This time, then, like all the times when it was better for me to be alone, I went to smoke my pipe a little distance from the hut like an old man; I opened the old almanac and it seemed to me that old man Jean was there, leaning over my shoulder and sliding his big black finger of hair along the lines. It was very soft, a little dull already by the weather. I would have liked to go knock on his door one evening.

Our life was more of a life of little wild beasts. We spent hours without speaking. My hair had grown so long that it fell with a mane down my back. She twisted hers and pricked them with a thorn to hold them to her neck. She liked to attach small strawberry pendants to her ears. It is also adorned with leaves: they enveloped it like a tunic. Me, under my frayed endless clothes, I was as thin as a wolf. We would have scared the little rich if we had been brought back to the city. But I had a knife and there was no one to tell us that the wood after all was someone's.

Former little beggars like us have a different notion of life than the children who went to school. It seemed to us that we could always have lived like this. Perhaps your father, Iule, and mine had done as we did, or else they had died in a distant land, walking in front of them, fierce and free. Or they had ended up on a scaffold. Who else could have told us what you and I were out of? The wind on this was silent: the little essences of the forest grow in the light and do not know from which tree they fell either. Our confidence in life was courageous and ingenuous. No one had taught us that the very strength of life within us. I feel that if the world had to be started anew, it would be with the seed of misery like us that we would start it all over again.

There was in the book a figure of the Zodiac which strangely represented a man on horseback, leaning an arrow at the curve of his bow. We had never seen such a man: he would have terrified us if he had appeared among the trees, rushing like an animal with horny feet. With his muscular arm, he held out the bow, reared up: he was doing something in town that I had seen do to those who, for a small penny, could buy a bow in the shops. The shape of the weapon immediately adapted to the thought of our hunts. I chose a flexible and hard branch, and having peeled the bark, I fixed at both ends a braided cord with the hemp threads that I had taken from the fabric of the bag. Then I cut arrows; and now I was like that terrible archer, with fate in my hands. Iule uttered her clamor: all the wood resounds with its frenzied wow. She wanted to wear the features, I held the bow in my fists; and we went down to the heart of the forest.

Iule in the shadows had frightening eyes: she walked close to me on tiptoe with a low laugh. Our ears were subtle and picked up the slightest rumors. Suddenly she made a sign: a squirrel, crouching on a branch, munching on pine cones. I bent the bow; the minute was anxious; and finally the arrow went off, toppled the nice animal, which for a moment tried to cling to the branches and then fell, its point straight to the gizzard.

Iule gave her savage cry. The little agony at our feet twitched in a flapping of the beautiful red tail. She thought he was dead, but as she put out her hand, with a last spasm the squirrel bit her finger. And then the life went away. I who by my will had killed this beast, I was not paying attention to Iule's anger: I remained bent over this little thing which was life and had played in the trees. But she was dancing around, trying to crush his head with her heels.

I tell him :

- Why are you hurting this beast since it is dead?

The teeth had barely entered her flesh and yet she was screaming as if she too was going to die. I withdrew the arrow and that day with the bow I killed two more birds. We were thus assured of never running out of food. Iule stopped lamenting; she proudly wore the trophy as the wife of a warrior tribal chief after a fight.

- If only, she said, you had a cap with a silver cord like the men on the tram in the city, there would be no one more handsome than you.

She spoke to me like a hero; my blood was running happily.

I took a liking to carnage; I became the little killer of the woods. Sometimes also, by throwing the knife, I could kill a rat or a rabbit. I had cut my hand for a long time by practicing on the trees. In the end I found the right way: I held the handle in my palm and with a stroke of my arm I threw the knife: the blade went deep. We then put the skins on the branches to dry. It was an idea that came to us thinking about winter. And one day she said to me:

- See, however, if you could kill one of the great beasts that come down to drink from the pond, I would make a beautiful skin coat for you like you see in the merchants over there.

But these were for me like the sacred hosts of the forest. Whenever I saw them from afar in small graceful leaps, I experienced the religious sensation of a life associated with the mystery of solitudes. After so long, I still cannot express this. They lived in herds with females with eyes of deep life, with friendly playful fawns. And Iule with his dangerous laugh, in a low voice always spoke to me about their fur.

I had carved a new pipe for myself in a birch knot. I took it with me on my hunts. I smoked dried leaves in there, savoring the taste of tinder. In the city, stinking tobacco waste was the delight of the poor. It was a joy for me to take big puffs, sitting at the foot of a tree like a real hunter. I used the time of the watch to draw, with the point of the knife, figures on my bow. This too, the first men had done like me. A hedgehog, in the cool hours, passed gently, like a light spirit of the earth. There were a lot of magpies and jays. The little crows were tender to eat. I killed a rooster of the woods once: we had never had such a feast and she kept the feathers that she wore on her head.

Iule sometimes went alone in the woods. I followed her, I saw her reflected in the pond. Leaning on her fists, she advanced her bust over the water and with her lips tried to kiss her image. She heard me laugh, jumped up to me and her eyes were feverish.

"Feel how my heart is beating," she said.

She had taken my hand and was pressing it between her small breasts. I didn't know what she meant. And suddenly, under the heat of my fingers, she began to tremble: nature tormented her young wild blood.

As we struggled, we rolled over the moss and it bit my neck. It would happen that I squeezed it a little too roughly: it fled into the thickets with a wounded cry. One day I called her in vain: she did not return to the hut. She loved to roll her head in my chest and listen to my life beat for a long time. It was such a deep mystery for us, the little spring which, drop by drop, hung still with its sound of eternity.

We did not know how long ago we had left the men. We now had other faces and other gestures. We begin again humanity according to our humble strength. Our life was violent and contemplative. I knew the hours of the day when the sap worked: it was the time of solar decline. Then the odors rose; the earth quivered; all the trees throbbed like swollen hearts, and in the morning new shoots came.

I saw the branch grow and the grass rise. The old almanac told me of the moons and the seasons; he initiated me into the prognoses which warn man of nature. I was the attentive and amazed little loner who listened to the birds singing. I learned to imitate their song by whistling; and with the days other birds arrived with other unknown voices.

Iule beside me listened to me: she found my sounds much more beautiful than their song. And I had not yet cut the pipes where I later became a skilled musician. She said to me:

- Sing like the one who makes burrows or like the one who makes di di di di.

We gave them naive names that matched their song.

There came some subtle sensations. We opened our arms to the wind; it was like a friendly thing that we lovingly press against us. I didn't know why I hugged the trees so tenderly. I thought I was breathing the whole sky, inhaling the air strongly. And on the ground with our hands we tried to grasp the moving gold of the lights: they were like large ruddy lizards, swift and furtive beasts that glided through the woods. Sometimes Iule untied her hair the color of rotten linen; with full fists she twisted them in the sun and said:

- See, isn't it the sun that I twist with my hair?

I loved so much looking at the green shadow life on her skin as she danced, holding the tip of her skirt in her fingers. She was an already cunning and lustful girl who seemed to know her empire. Her skirt was rising higher and higher and she was laughing mute. I laughed too, with another laugh, because I remembered that she had been naked in the pond. I thought she had an idea she wasn't telling me.

One day, sitting near the house, I was reading in the book. The path creaked under his feet, I looked up; she was there in front of me, circling around, her skirt in her hands, with mannered graces. Who had taught him that? Through her narrowed eyelids, she was giving me a sharp look.

- See how I dance, she said.

I thought of another little girl who, in a suburb of the city, once danced to the sound of a clarinet and a drum. This one also had a beautiful dress, oh! a very short dress, more like a skirt of old, dirty and faded gauze, but covered with gold threads. As she pivoted on her worn-out pumps with her purple-red undershirt, her black, clenched little hand took kisses from her mouth, which she threw at the audience, common people, big and small thugs like me. I will never forget the amazement left by this pitiful human puppet. I say to Iule:

- There was once a little girl dancing. I had never seen more beautiful.

I felt a singular pleasure to speak to him thus. Iule suddenly stopped turning; she came over me, her fists raised, and asked if I liked this one too. I then, defiantly because of the anger in her eyes, laughing that I would gladly have come to the forest with her. I amused myself by his jealous sorrow with a feeling of independence, thus expressing that after all I was master of following my taste. Immediately she pulled her hair back and shouted that if I ever brought another girl to the woods, she would kill her.

- Yes, there you go, I'll crush him with my heels. I'll tear his heart out with my teeth.

Then she threw herself on my neck and now she was crying, with a fierce and tender little heart.

- No, you see, you shouldn't do that. Say, Old Man, would you really do that someday? I assure you, you would kill me too.

I felt an evil pride that it was suddenly so humbly mine as a prey, like a little beast with beak and nails that my valor had tamed. I felt I was the master of his life. I would have only had to take it under the armpits and throw it on the grass.

A fire ate my entrails; I looked at her so furiously that she got scared and cried:

- Little old man ! how terrible you look!

Was she really shaking? She hid her head in her hands and said to me gently:

- Do whatever you want with me.

And I, seeing her soft and submissive, shrugged my shoulders without answering her as if now I no longer knew what she wanted from me. I took out my almanac; I spelled out, with my finger on the letters, the parable of the old man in the desert. I was happy with sad joy, feeling his little hand on my shoulder as I read. Every time I opened the pages, I had the feeling that the book too was a force like wind and thunder, but a force for good. Something good and divine emanated from it as when, at the school of the good teacher, I believed to see God rising with the gesture of which he made the ball turn in front of the candle, saying to us: This is the earth and this the sun. I did not dream of wondering by what miracle the ideas had descended and froze there in letters. I would have been astonished if someone had told me about the man who with a small pliers took them in a locker and put them one after the other like the pieces of a game of patience . Perhaps in me I had a little feeling that this was a natural thing of life, as it comes from fingernails to fingers and hair to skin.

The forest was red: it passed a cold through the thinned trees. Iule no longer went down to the heart of the forest with me. I went hunting alone, killing a squirrel here and there with arrows. I came home wet, my half-naked flesh all cold under my rags. Even on sunny days, the shade remained damp. So she imagined sewing together the animal skins that we would dry on branches. With the point of the knife I pierced small holes in them; she passed cords removed from the weft of the sack and which she braided firmly. We didn't stop laughing the first time we put on this strange garment. We appeared to ourselves like beasts out of the thicket and now, under the warm wild pelisse, we no longer feared the cold or the rain.

Patiently I began to cut hooves for Iule from large branches; we had brought similar ones to the hamlet. But while I finished digging the second of the hooves, the blade of my knife became blunt: I would have preferred to cut my finger. Our whole life was in this knife: it was the essential tool without which I could neither have rebuilt the hut nor made myself an arch. And, with the shattered blade between my fingers, I stood there quite pale, pondering what would happen to us if another chip were to bite it. I only used it with extreme caution.

Having descended that day towards the pond, we perceived a noise which was not yet known to us. Loud shots at regular intervals beat in the great silence of the forest. Iule said to me:

- It's like when I put my head on your chest and hear your heart beating.

The heart of the forest also seemed to leap in these deep shocks. It was frightening and distant as if, at a great distance, men were fighting with the forest. In the humid and heavy air, the sound became dull and at times seemed to rise from below the earth. It didn't last long, it was choked like the beating of a heart under a thick sheet and yet it was terrible.

He fills us with fear; we could not doubt that men had come into the forest and were doing something mysterious and dreadful there. The beatings lasted until nightfall and then they started again in the misty morning. It seemed to us that all the wood was shaking. I say to Iule:

- If they come to take us, I have my knife.

Yet it was more of an affected bravery. Now that the man was once again approaching us, all the more dangerous because we were still hidden, I was less confident. Iule, in her sheer courage, was admirable.

- You will kill them with your knife, she said fiercely, and I will shoot arrows. And then with my bare feet I'll dance on their hearts like after the squirrel bites me.

She spoke like a real warrior, like a girl from the wild tribes. We went down together into the forest; I went ahead, holding my knife in my hands; she followed me, carrying the bow. The blows in the rainy day had died down: sometimes we ceased to hear them altogether; and they were far away, on the other side of the forest. We tried in vain to orient ourselves when they resumed. We walked with great caution as if now we were the game.

One day of the other year, taking small steps, we had discovered the camp: behind the huts there were hairy men who moved with subtle rhythms that before that time we had ignored. These, after all, were benevolent beings in their big, mute faces. And we wondered what other unknown worker so furiously made the heart of the forest moan. Suddenly Iule had pale eyes in the shadow of the thicket:

- Say, Old Man. What if they weren't men? What if it was a beast like the one that once passed through the street and was as high as a house?

She had often spoken to me of an animal that was led to play like an actor in a circus. I believe it was an elephant; but then neither she nor I knew the name yet. The idea that such a terrible animal lived in the forest made us, that evening, desert the hut: we climbed up to the beech and, keeping ourselves entwined in the warmth of our squirrel skins, we slept in the shelter where our nights had been so often rocked in the summer wind.

At dawn the forest quivered again, and now it seemed the blows had drawn closer. Our life remained troubled with the fear of a secret enemy who always surely advanced and attacked the wood from all sides. Towards noon of the day the depths roared; the air was torn with a horrible crash, after which there reigned a great silence; and now I no longer believed it was a beast that made such a noise.

- I assure you, Iule, it is indeed the men and they cut down the forest. When the big branch fell one night, it was also like a thunderclap.

She looked at me laughing:

- Oh ! she said, maybe there are boys like you among them, Old Man.

Why is she telling me that? His nostrils were pounding. She no longer spoke of dancing on their hearts with her bare heels. I would have liked to bite his neck. I say :

- If there's a boy like me ...

And there you are, I remained silent afterwards, with something in me that I could not have expressed; and maybe also Iule had thought of this thing.

The next day she said to me quietly:

- We will go in front of us as long as we have seen.

She's right, I thought; you will then know what you have to do. We had come with the bow and the knife in our hands: however if at that moment a human form had appeared, I would have thrown my knife to the ground.

We walked for a long time: the blows resounded more distinctly and with each stroke the forest moaned. We were light, confident; we sang, holding hands. But a cock of the woods, in plumage of copper and fire, with a loud cry arose from a thicket. I shot an arrow; she wandered off, and almost immediately a rabbit stuck in her bush. We forgot the men.

Breathlessly, we watched to see if the rabbit was going to exit through another passage a short distance away. There only came a squirrel which to look at us advanced to the end of a branch. Again I raised the bow and took aim. The cunning critter circled around the trunk and I too, with my bow outstretched, spun around, waiting for the moment. Finally the arrow went off, the squirrel rolled. In our joy, we danced around his death. With our animal skins, we looked really terrible; she was pushing her wow wow; my cries made the birds fly away. Our madness stirred all the wood. It seemed to us that distant voices answered our clamors.

- Believe me, she said, this is the way to go.

She was showing me the West.

We listened: the voices were silent and once again the heart of the trees was ringing under the blows.

We had lived in the solitude of this forest for months; I no longer knew how a man's face was made. My eyes looked fiercely in front of me. Our hooves in our hands, we ran in the direction of the voices. I had put the warm little body of the squirrel under a bed of leaves; I had planted a branch next to it in order to recognize the place when we would come back to take it back. And now a secret force was attracting us, relaxing the springs of the race beneath us. I thought: maybe there are girls like Iule there; but I didn't tell Iule. A smell of burnt wood erupted; the depths were vaporized with blue spirals gently carried by the wind. It was a smoke like the one that one day had drawn us to the huts of the tribe. She felt the shelter, the family meal after the working day; she caressed our hearts so softly when, at nightfall, she came towards us, at the edge of the clay desert where all day long, under the blazing sun, we had toiled! We sucked it up as after a long hunger we eat bread. Neither of them thought about our little hut in the heart of the forest.

A young man's voice sang and I took Iule's hands; she hugged mine; we wanted to cry. A vast discovery opened the forest towards the depths. We were afraid a dog would bark. We were crawling under the trees, me holding the knife in my hands. I would have killed the dog. And then suddenly at a little distance, the singing began again. Men under the trees were talking: their voices, in the heavy silence, with the weight of the forest on them, were unheard of, as if they rose from the depth of a well. They hurt us deliciously.

Lying in the low vegetation, we stood up on our fists, watching the huts smoke in the clearing. There were two, half made of butted planks, half paved with clods of earth; and they had no other opening than the door. They were much more primitive than the brickmaker's house.

My God ! How suddenly my sympathy arose for these men who had made a roof like our roof! No doubt they too lived on free and wild prey like us. How many were there? Did they have their wives with them? My heart was beating against the earth. Something sometimes moved in one of the huts, a vague shape we couldn't recognize. An old man, very tall, was hitting the foot of a beech with the ax. With each blow, he bent down, threw the iron with all his height into the already deep gash; and then with an effort of his arm he would pull it out and start hitting again. Han was not immediately heard. I envied the quiet strength of this man. No doubt the others were farther away: you could hear the blows of their ax and you could not see them.

Once again the happy voice arose. She came from the back of the hut and then she walked up to the threshold. And now a young man was there, his arms crossed, in the attitude of rest between two jobs, looking with his pale pupils towards the forest. He wore leather gaiters on his legs; her curly head clung tightly to her broad shoulders. Iule, upright on her fists, looked at him with the eyes of a little wolf.

- This one is more beautiful than you! she breathed into my neck.

- Well ! go with him. I will return to the woods alone.

If she had done so, perhaps I would have raised my knife to her. I was very sweet and sad. I too admired this young boy: I would have liked to have had him for a brother.

No doubt he heard our voices. He had the fixed, hard gaze of men accustomed to gazing into the night from the woods; and he craned his neck a little, curious, astonished. We saw each other uncovered: yet we did not have the strength to flee, nailed to the spot by those eyes that never left us.

Another, after all, would have experienced the same surprise on seeing two creatures appear from the earth, clothed in bleeding skins and whose faces alone had retained a human appearance. With a bound he sprang forward, split the clearing; his laughter sounded like a bark; and our hooves in our hands, now also we were running like hunted beasts. We were ahead; our bare feet gave us more agility. He lost our trail.

The moon rose. Neither Iule nor I spoke no more: perhaps she was thinking of this magnificent young man. In the pale night, silvery silks slid in long, wet streaks. The whole forest seemed like a dream in an immense peace of sleep. Finally the shelter was seen: we were there in the very heart of the silence. And Iule, with her head against my shoulder, was a softly passed out, throbbing little thing. The hours no longer existed.

Voices. Laughs. A stifled uproar. Our eyes reopened and it was morning that came slowly with a troop of men strangely bending down and watching us wake up. There were three, already old, very straight under the years, and the fourth was this boy who, from the bottom of the clearing, had rushed towards us. Iule, with a cry, gathered himself under the leaves. I was standing, I felt my knife in my pocket.

The old people looked at us with a somewhat reassuring look. But the young man laughed as he showed them our animal skins.

- Here. They were sitting at the edge of the clearing when I gave chase. I thought he had come from the monkeys in the forest.

Iule stirred under the leaves, amused at the idea. She laughed and said to me:

- Oh ! Little Old Man, do you hear? They took us for monkeys.

Sometimes men settled down at the crossroads: they had small marmosets with sick eyes, decked out in troop shoulders or marquise frills. She and I often took pleasure in seeing them dance tug of war or maneuver a gun. I proudly say to this boy:

- We are men like you.

- Yes, my faith! he cried. They have arms and faces like us.

And he didn't stop looking at Iule. One of the old men saw our wood reserves, the skins drying on the branches, the stones on which we were cooking our prey. He pointed to the forest with a broad gesture and said harshly:

- They're the ones who break the young trees. They kill the beasts.

I rested on him with resolute eyes and replied quietly:

- The forest is ours. There was no one here when we came.

So this old man laughed too.

- They say the forest is theirs!… My family and I have been cutting down trees for a hundred years and not even a leaf belongs to us.

The young man leaned over me and gently asked me who this red-haired girl was. I thought she was going to answer him like a bricklayer:

- This one is Old Man and I am his wife.

She only said to me:

- Speak to him, you, as you think you should speak.

Cunning and mistrust arose. After all, by what right were these people questioning us?

- It's Iule, I say, and I am called Little Old Man. I won't say more.

They exchanged a few more words among themselves; then the older one took a step.

- Here. There is bread here. If you have a heart, you will come to work. We will arrange for the rest.

Bread ! Once again the temptation arose. This one had spoken like the old man among the bricklayers. I turned to Iule and then all the free life of the forest was in front of me: I dared not look at her. It throbbed against my chest. She whispered in my ear: "Bread, Old Man!" Think about it! "

I tell him :

- It will be as you like. Tell you.

I would have liked her to show me the forest while shaking her head; but she got up, she put her hand on the young boy's arm, laughing.

"I'll go with you, if he wants to," she said.

This heart of Iule was full of detours. She spoke as if I had decided that we would follow these unknown men. When I was a poor boy in the cities, I threw a stone in the air. Depending on whether it fell, I did one thing or the other. And now it was she who was my destiny.

So we left the hut. Goshawks were lovingly sobbing. A blue mist was smoking over the forest. All the herbs sparkled. Never had the morning seemed more beautiful to me. And I had fastened my shoes by a liana to my neck, Iule was wearing her beautiful dress rolled up in the bag. This is how we reached the logging camp.

The young man pushed open the door of the plank house. He happily said to Iule:

- There is only you woman here. The others are in the forest further on.

Then he cut us some bread. My God ! the taste had always stuck with us; however, she and I thought we were eating it for the first time.

It was the beginning of our old life with men. The instinct of humanity once again prevailed, made us accept the vague social bond with which this tribe remained united in the depths of the woods. It was made up of simple and rough souls who had the silences, the dormant life of little pools of sun in the hollow of the ravines. They lived among the trees, woody and indestructible, with a wild sap and tender pith. A lasting companionship in the green heart of solitudes united them with a tenacious affection without words. They didn't feel the need to say anything to each other, all having the same ideas and no words to express them. Which of them was the first to come to the forest with his ax, they ignored: it was an ancient tradition that was being lost in the very age of the silve. Their generations had worn themselves out always striking the great oaks to the heart: where they passed, rivers of sap flowed and did not diminish the inexhaustible fountains of life. Like the bricklayers, they walked in front of them, doing an obscure work, striking blows in all directions which resounded against the dies of the earth. They did not understand the destiny that drove them to work tirelessly for the cities.

Most had not gone beyond the limit of the hamlets. Sometimes they would go there looking for women and get married there. The nuptials were brief and ended under the blue arches of the forest, in the night of the huts. When one of them died, we nailed it between freshly sawn planks and together, taking turns, we carried it to the cemetery, far away. These were the only chores that attached them to the lives of other men. They were gentle and concealed, a little sad.

Iacq was the boy's name. He taught me how to handle the ax. After the tree had fallen, the branches had to be cut down; the big ones went through a saw; the averages were bundled into falourdes; the twigs formed bundles and brooms. The master loggers only struck the tree at the foot.

Iacq tells me:

- I'll teach you how to cut down oaks.

This young man was a great force of life. When that one laughed, the birds were silent, all the silence of the forest was broken. He was a true son of the woods, and yet he did not have the taciturnity of the other children of the tribe. His gaiety as a healthy and robust man stood out against their deaf and withdrawn life. I admired his calm vigor as he threw the ax, arched over his loins, torso twisted to one side. The iron fell, made a large wound, foam and wet from having struck in green blood. Iacq seemed to bang in the joyful intoxication of his strength, muscles wired up to equal the powerful ribs of the beech. His ax vibrated, with the hum of a big fly when heard from afar. Sometimes he would cut off his hard work with a song sung at the top of his voice, or else he would whistle, imitating birds.

I did not yet know the suffering of trees: the blows of the ax made me want to strike in my turn. One day, as he jokingly challenged me, I picked up the heavy mass; I threw it on the fly; she fell down beside the gash, practiced deep marrow. I had the giddiness of having entered the iron in a human chest, in a life of gold and blood. The tree quivers with all its foliage: a muffled noise was lost in the silences of the forest. And now I was no longer unaware of my strength. Iacq stopped laughing and said:

- You will be a lumberjack.

There we were, in the cup, eight men and Iule. The rest of the tribe scattered from glade to glade. They had huts like ours: there were more of them and women prepared their meals. It was Iule who was responsible for cleaning our camp. She lit the fire, then ran the water over the coffee maker. A decoction of chicory soaked our brown bread during the day. The smoke rose under the trees, wadded up in light blue flakes which dissipated only slowly, rolling in the wind into the valleys. In the evening, the flame darted higher: Iule then cooked the potatoes. It was, along with pork rind, our usual food. These forest people knew no other. Iule and I were surprised that having the fruits and the animals of the forest, they content themselves with these simple foods. Their probity was fierce: they lived in voluntary poverty, in the vast abundance of the earth. None of them thought that after all this one is for the men who toil and suffer on its side. They respected the ancient defenses, subject to their fate, valiant and naked. Once I killed a young rabbit with a stick and brought it back to the hut. Big-toothed Iacq ate it. The old people were not happy. I understood that only we, Iule and I, had known the free life. Once I killed a young rabbit with a stick and brought it back to the hut. Big-toothed Iacq ate it. The old people were not happy. I understood that only we, Iule and I, had known the free life. Once I killed a young rabbit with a stick and brought it back to the hut. Big-toothed Iacq ate it. The old people were not happy. I understood that only we, Iule and I, had known the free life.

At dawn, the work began. The first shiver of the day slipped over the summits, a creepy vapor fluffed the damp shadow. And then the light descended, cool, still cloudy like a great wave after the valves raised. The depths remained misty for a long time; step by step a purple mist was iridescent in the filtered sun, oblique and mobile like oscillating columns. The ax leaped like a golden puck. The blows made the sky tremble above the trees.

Noon brought a truce: a heavy sleep weighed down; the buzzing of the big flies hovered; and the men, lying in the cool of the moss, with their large collapsed torsos, themselves resembled fallen trunks. One of the old men then clapped his hands: we cut down until the end of the day. Then the shade freshened, blue as in the morning; the mystery descended. My God ! these were sensations that we had known for a long time; and yet, mingled with this tribal life, they always seemed new to us. Iule, between the time of meals, tied the falourds with her rags and I sometimes let the ax rest, listening to the magpies laughing or the woodpecker neighing.

Iacq one day gave me a pipe and some tobacco. I liked him because of his gaiety and his strength and yet I distrusted him, I could not say why. Perhaps he had a look on Iule which was not the same when he turned it towards me. I didn't think of explaining this feeling to myself. The gift of the pipe binds us. I was really happy to smoke like the old people around me.

"See how good he is, this boy," said Iule to me. He shares with you what he has and you hardly talk to him.

I would have liked to tell her that she was paying too much attention to him; they often went off together to laugh behind the huts. And then, tugging on the pipe, I shrugged my shoulders as if that was a secret that did not concern me. I was not jealous: it seemed natural to me that she would find him more handsome than me, the Old Man.

Iacq, moreover, would not have put one step in front of the other to please him. He treated her like a strange little beast that cried and cried without cause. Once, as he joked about her skinny legs, she bit his hand and ran to hide in the woods.

His annoyance lasted two days; she told me she hated him; she wanted to go back to the hut with us. And then she laughed again with him. He seemed much more cordial when she wasn't there. I believe that in this Iacq's mind, there was the idea that Iule was a bit of a living toy. He had gone to seek her in the heart of the woods; he had done no other than a wild man in the hunt for females. She was to him like a young prey whom he loved to laugh and have fun with, a prey with a soul other than his own. Yes, I think that was his idea.

I developed a taste for the profession. When the tree was very high and when it collapsed it had smashed the surrounding trees, I put my fangs and climbed up to the head. With great turns of the ax, I undermined the branches. I was up there like the woodpecker that kicks the sapwood and brings out the insects. I used to make the birds fly. I dominated the silences of the forest.

It was again, after all, a wild life: I had wood pigeons and jays for companions. And a feeling that I had known among bricklayers came back to me, the pride of not being useless and of earning my bread, as it was said in the old almanac. In the evening, after the meal, while smoking my pipe on the doorstep, I was really aware of having become a man.

Now we also knew the Sunday rest. That day the axles and saws were idle. The loggers went up to the high camps; sometimes they walked to the hamlets.

Once Iacq told me:

- You who can read, read in the book.

None of the tribesmen had learned to spell the letters. The mothers, crossing their hands, had taught them prayer in their infancy. It was the simple prayer of bread: they recited it before and after meals. The good man Jean also said it aloud before starting the class and together the little ones repeated it, in a low hum which dragged for a moment under the smoky joists. Iule and I had forgotten about her since our return to the forest.

The forest, under the wind and the rains, was stripped. In the morning the earth creaked under the frost and now every Sunday I read aloud in the book for Iacq and the old people. I spelled first, with a finger on the letters, as the old master did. There were words I never came to terms with; but I tried to grasp the meaning and then, line by line, I read. This little house where a humble ignorant boy raised his voice and said eternal things in naked solitude, had its beauty. I didn't understand it until later. If others, according to their strength, went away, as I was doing there, to spread the good word among the men of the hamlets and the woods, humanity would gain new souls there.

We worked until the heavy snow. The frost did not stop the axles: they struck the heart of the great trees with the death of the sap. A silence filled the harsh air; he was torn apart only by the grilling of jays and the hoarse clamor of crows. The men of nature do not feel the cold: their blood remains young and warm under the ice cubes. As soon as my hands had touched the ax, a force of life flowed in them, I struck my blows straight, warmed to the marrow. Ah! Iule! what a joy it was for us now, the great winter forest with its crystallizations that filigrated the smallest branches on a par with the silversmiths glittering over there on the merchants' shelves! Neither you nor I had ever seen anything more beautiful. It seemed to us that our heart beat louder near the rigid heart of nature, in all this frozen stillness of the old chills of summer. We were the warmth of ancient humanities surviving the cataclysms of the world. The races cried out for life in us when around us the appearances of death reigned.

Then the great snows swirled: we had to make our way through the avalanche, fall back on the high camps. The tribe, the large family scattered in the cups, reformed under roofs more solid than the precarious shelter of the huts. There were six large huts, with the bread ovens, the goat barn, the pig stall. A sort of human nucleus lived there with a common life on the edge of the yards. Mothers were breastfeeding their children near the large wood fires. The ancestors helped knead the rye or repair the clothes. Old men, former loggers, crippled with years and ailments, parched to the bone, expiated the immemorial outrages of the forest. These dragged along strange infirmities which made one think of the ganglia of trees tormented in their growth.

Alcohol was everyone's great temptation: it was banned in the camp; they compensated themselves in the villages. Iacq himself, that honest boy, once came home drunk: he had met other guys with whom he had fought to the point of blood. He would have perished in the snows if one of the old people, who had gone to drink in the canteens with him, had not brought him back on his shoulders. Iule admired him. She said to me strangely:

- You, Old Man, you wouldn't have done that for me.

She was talking there as if a girl had been the cause of the brawl.

The huts, moreover, were not idle in the winter of the forest. We made brooms with the brooms. Small branches were used to weave baskets and planters that, towards spring, merchants came to buy. It was the same industry as among the men of the desert; but these used wicker.

We also repaired the tools. In the evening, the crassets lit up. I opened the book; the finger on the lines, I read. A light was in my eyes while little times, by taking myself back, I naively developed the maxims or commented on the stories in my own way. What a beautiful audience it was, those rough faces tanned by tans, these souls of simple climbs to the folds of their foreheads, strained in the effort to understand! I thought the whole forest was listening to me.

However, a misunderstanding remained between these people from the huts and us. They had the regular life of a tribe fixed in the forest. Iule and I were suspicious beings for them, escaped from the cities and came to hide in the woods. They felt the muffled distrust of creatures resigned to serfdom towards the free children of life. Was it me who was inferior to them, with my fierce instinct?

I also had a soul that was both wilder and more tender, a soul that did not immediately see the evil around me. I had thought I hated men: I felt no deep resentment against them; however there was between humanity and me our old martyred life.

Iacq was the only man in the camps that I really loved: I would have gone with him to the end of the forest. If only he had wanted to call Iule less often to laugh with her behind the boxes, I would have been quite his friend. She still had blood on her cheeks afterwards; the laughter left her trembling.

- Oh ! she said, this Iacq is such a strange boy… You can't imagine what he's telling me!

She looked at me, started laughing again and I never knew what Iacq had said to her. I no longer loved this young man with the same confident heart, although after all, with this crazy Iule, the wrongs perhaps were not entirely on his side. Besides, he laughed with all the women. These between them spoke of a girl he knew in the hamlets.

One day one of the men came back from the forest and said:

- The snows have melted.

We gathered the clothes, we tied the loaves in the sheets. The small troop one morning took the road to the huts.

With the days there came birds, the first timid songs of the year. The skies were high; a young, male sun lit up the regrowth of the leaves. My joy was virgin and fresh as the awakening of nature. The whole forest sang in me and Iacq under the trees sang with the gaiety of a young giant. Now, when they looked at each other, Iule and him, it was to laugh together with muffled voices as if I no longer mattered to them. Or else he motioned to her and they both went behind the hut. He spoke to me softly; he gave me tobacco more often; and Iule too rubbed against me with more tenderness. The two seemed to agree to put to sleep my suspicions about something that must have remained unknown to me. Never had she been so caressing; she had the strokes of a playful little pussy.

Why does she tell me one day that she loved me better than Iacq? His impulse was spontaneous and sincere, although I had asked nothing of him. If she had told me instead that she preferred this boy to me, I would have dragged her by the hair. It was only then that I began to suspect that they were hiding something from me. I didn't believe in anything wrong, it was rather the feeling that between her and him there was an understanding to surrender freely to their cheerful mood. Iule loved pleasure and I was just the sullen little old man. If I could have suspected what they were always laughing about together, I wouldn't have been bored. But then, when I was there, they both pursed their lips and stopped laughing.

It happened several times that Iule herself went and took the tobacco and stuffed my pipe with it. I didn't know if it was Iacq who sent it or if she did it on her own, and then what right did she have over Iacq's tobacco?

- No, you see, I said once to him, I will no longer smoke his tobacco. It's an idea I have. You can tell him from me.

Iule immediately began to shout bitterly that Iacq's tobacco was mine, that everything else in the hut was in common.

"I don't like him," I replied. This is my idea. I have nothing else to tell you.

- Iacq is such a strange boy. He might get mad and you're not the strongest.

- I planted the ax right in the heart of the oak tree. He can come, I'm not afraid.

No doubt she reported my words to Iacq, for he came the next day to offer me tobacco himself, and as I put his hand away, he said to me without anger:

- Why are you doing this insult to me? I assure you, I offered it to you with a good heart.

I should have turned my back on him, since it was my idea not to accept anything from him and I had told Iule. But he seemed sincere and spoke to me like a man determined not to hold a grudge. My courage failed me; I put out my hand, he squeezed it in his. And now they were both laughing once again.

One morning with Iacq I had won a cut back. I was there in a tree, ax working in the tall branches. He, too, at a short distance, struck at the heart of a beech tree. The iron sounded after the iron, the blows answered each other like voices in the young life of the forest. For two days he had stopped talking to me; he had a crease of will in his eyebrows. I did not yet know what project was maturing in this deceitful boy. We had therefore come together to the cup, without saying anything to each other; and then we had played with our ax. The new sap was intoxicating me, my blood was rushing through my arteries. Each of my blows resounded in me and made me dizzy as if my life adhered to that of the tree, as if I myself were one of the swollen branches of the green flow that carried spring.

My strength fell, I would be rolled down from the oak, in the pain of anguish that was strangling me. He's gone to join Iule, I thought. And such a movement of pain and jealousy, I hadn't felt it yet. I let myself slide, the hard bark grating my limbs; and with my ax in my hands, I in turn ran in front of me. He entered the plank house, called Iule, and she was not there. Then from the threshold he shouted Iule several times! Iule! slowly, turning towards the edge of the clearing. She appeared behind the trees with a load of wood; from afar she was smiling at him. Now I was hiding, crushing my heart against the earth.

- See, he said, I was looking for you. I left the forest to tell you something.

And once again he rushed forward, a wild laugh in his teeth. She had dropped the wood bag she was carrying and was sitting there, weeping softly in her hands.

- No, she said, I don't want to hear that. You've told me too many times already. And yet, I assure you, when you tell me, I am dying of pleasure.

The air was light and a small distance separated us: I could clearly hear their words. Iacq now shrugged and looked at her with cold eyes under his raised eyebrows. I thought, "If he just puts his hand on her, I'll leap, I'll kill him with the ax." I didn't know what to do with Iule next. I stayed like that for a little while, stretched like a bowstring, biting my hands until I bleed so as not to cry out. All my strength had returned to me, a cold and bandaged energy, in the sly expectation of the event. I wanted to know finally why they always laughed together. And it was also another torturing and evil feeling, a cloudy joy to bleed my life there, in a thirst for impure suffering.

Iacq sat down next to her for a moment, hissing his teeth and nodding his head. Sometimes, before cutting down the ax, he lingered thus whistling, measuring by the power of the tree the force of the effort. The blow was all the more terrible afterwards. But Iule suddenly withdrew her hand from her eyes and looked at him defiantly: she had looked at me like that before. And now, with the clamor of an animal, he pushed her by the shoulders, ate her mouth greedily, lying on her with all his giant mass.

- Little old man ! cried Iule.

There you go, that thing could have happened. I would have killed this helpless man, listening to the original instinct, and then never again would I have touched an ax without seeing him lying on the ground in his blood. So I ran to Iacq brandishing the ax: if he had had a knife, we would have fought until nightfall. But, getting up, he crossed his arms and said to me quietly:

- Well, you saw it. Strike, since you are the lucky one.

Iule too, in her cowardice as a woman, cried:

- Yes, yes, hit him, I won't stop you.

It was the first disturbing movement of nature. She trembled in front of my cocked arm. She felt me victorious and turned against the vanquished. Other women had done this before her. However, this man had desired her with a warm passion of blood and youth. O Iule! strange violent and mobile heart, he had said the words of love to you! She saw him in his calm beauty, proudly offering herself to death and no doubt she admired him, because suddenly, seizing my arm:

- I do not want. If you missed him, you wouldn't miss him.

So I threw my ax with all my strength. It sank deep into the earth, in front of Iacq. And I say to Iule:

- It's not so much because of you as because he came without his ax.

He looked at me, his eyes straight.

- I don't like to owe my life to you, the youngest. And yet I say it: If you love this girl, take her; I will not put one step in front of the other to dispute it with you.

If, like me, he had conquered Iule over misery and pain, he would have preferred death. But his flesh alone neighed: For his male lusts, Iule had been nothing but the booty of hunting, the temptation and the pursuit of game in the acrid smell of the forest. He walked away whistling; I saw him take the road to the cup again; and, as time went by, the little song, soft as the flute of the wind, sank with him under the trees. Now I was sobbing, my head in my fists, collapsed among the ferns, without pride and weak as a child. All my anger was gone, I didn't hold it against Iule or that wild boy. It was a soft pain, a dull ache of my fibers, with the same cry that kept coming back:

- Why did you do that, Iule?

However, I could not have said what a bad thing Iule had done. She stroked my hair: she had sat down next to me and held my head in her knees.

- If you mean I laughed with that boy, yes, I was wrong, she said. He constantly called me from behind the hut and there he hugged me with all his strength. He still wanted to kiss me. I defended myself as best I could and laughed. Once he told me a strange thing that you, Old Man, you had not told me yet. You see, I will not repeat it to you.

She spoke to me honestly: she had the innocence of a girl that the man's kiss only touched. I dared not ask him if he had taken her mouth to his lips. My heart was once again mortally wounded. And then slowly, hiding my game to better capture his confidence, I laughed.

- Iule, tell me, how did he do it? As he did, I too will.

- The other morning, he threw my head back like that. I thought he wanted to bite me.

- Like that, you say?

I stood up on my fists and with fury I took her mouth between my teeth. She cried, quite pale:

- You hurt me ! Please, if you do it again, do it less hard.

But now I rolled her under me, I banged her neck against the ground, I said quietly in my jealous madness:

- You see, you too could kill you, horrible Iule!

She stiffened, her eyes widened with terror and charmed:

- Go, you can if it's your pleasure: I will not cry any more.

And she was there like a little martyr, her arms hanging down to her sides, with a happy face, looking like she was waiting for the holy death. I don't remember how it happened that suddenly my hands relaxed. I was crying, I was laughing, I was tenderly holding her lips, saying:

- Do I still hurt you like this?

I had never known such happiness. Her mouth tasted like hot fruit. I would have liked to die drinking its fresh juice. Iule had closed his eyes and uttered light cries. If, however, Iacq, that day, had not returned to the hut, I would have been ignorant for a long time yet that I loved Iule with the heart of a man. Nature had finally uttered her cry in me.

She said to me kindly now:

- Why didn't you do it before him? I waited for you so long, I was still sick of something you didn't want to understand.

I too, Iule, I cried and sobbed in the wood, I touched my flesh, I thought I touched it with your hands. A light flooded us: the night was torn apart, and I no longer hid myself from it. I naively told him from what evil I too had suffered. It was a very pure moment on the verge of knowledge, with the tremor of virginity between us, like a last defense. She returned my kisses and sighed.

- Believe me. There is something else the boy always told me about.

In her ingenuous torment, she was like Eve blushing with an unknown fire while laughing she showed Adam the shadow of the tree like a finger on her side. The good master had told us this story.

At this moment one of the old hucha insulting us. We were disturbed to see ourselves in broad daylight in the clearing, with our naked souls on our faces.

O Iule! This man was there! He saw us kissing!

It seemed to me that he had stolen part of our secret from us. I hated him, I suddenly hated all men once again. But she attracted me laughing, in her free instinct of love.

- Let him scream. Am I really not your wife now? If he comes, I'll tell him he's not past the spot where you planted the ax.

The wild passion for wood was unleashed. I say to Iule:

- Listen. It's over between men and us. You and I will go until there is nothing around us but the green night of the woods. I'm sleepy of you. It's been so long since you slept next to me, with your head against my chest.

The man left. And then Iule, slipping behind the trees, entered the house. She tied her clothes and mine in the bag. I picked up the ax and carried it over my shoulder. So we left the camp.

Like the seed pushed by the wind, we went ahead of us. Iacq had often told me about the great forest which extended towards the west. This one, Iule and I did not know her yet. "You see," he said to me, "walking every day from dawn to night, it would take weeks to go around it. No living man, having entered it, left it. It was already afternoon; we were heading towards the curve of the sun. At the edge of the forest, bushy essences appeared, plant life enveloped us like a sea, and now a weariness, an infinite languor had seized us. We took a few steps and then our mouths sought each other. A very gentle fire was consuming us. The earth around us also came into love.

"I won't go any further," she said. See how my heart beats.

My God ! What madness ! I dropped the ax and there I was, kissing her little throat with a big cold tremor. Our flesh cried out to each other, palpitating, wounded, the divine torment of substance, all the duration of the races in us from the origins.

I say one last time weakly:

- Do I hurt you like this?

A light wind rustled, waved the leaves on us. There were only two creatures left who had exchanged the sacred gift of life.

O little Iule! That was why you and I, the first day, we had come to the tree, from the depths of the horrible misery of the cities. Destiny had started for us with the exchange of a piece of bread and now we had given each other life through time without limits. I cry softly to evoke the incredible hour.

Iule! Iule!

That night in the forest where all with your dear hot life, you were in my hand! This night of stars and shivers under the oak, with dew sheets on our bed, with the cool mouth of the wind drinking our sighs from our mouths! The shadow of gold and azure palpitated, tender and fierce; and we were now, you and I, the same thing of life. We no longer knew where one was starting to become the other. I gave you the name of woman for the first time. I kept calling you: My wife, and you said to me: Little Old Man, with a voice that I had not yet heard. And then the morning dawned: you put your hand in front of your face.

We didn't go far into the forest that day or the next day. We took a few steps and fell close to each other. It seemed to me that we would never have finished knowing each other. I drank his life from his lips like a spring, and then I was more thirsty. My blood spun like a fiery grindstone. I was dizzy with all the unknown of her love: a light fold to her skin and the fine hair in her armpits were like so many little sisters of her that she gave me after having given herself. She did not stop giving of herself and she was a new Iule in every part of her life that touched my mouth and my hands. She was much more a virgin than when her throat swelled for the first time, when she innocently rested her neck on my shoulder, in the night of the hut.

My God ! could such a thing be? You were now my life even as the sap and the bark do not separate and make the same living rumor. You took my head in your hands, you pressed it against your breasts and I listened to live my life with the deep waves of yours. They stuck drop by drop like twin waters in the same basin and they made the sound of a sea. My eyes were drunk to see the small dimple of shadow throbbing which was the pulse of your heart. You in turn put your ear to the place where my skin was beating. Gently you pinched it between your lips, you sucked it like a fruit.

- See, I eat your heart, you said.

It was only a tickle and it seemed to me that your whole heart was coming to your lips, that it rose from the bottom of me sucked by this movement of the mouth from which you would have emptied the juice of a ripe plum. Sometimes you and I stopped talking, overwhelmed under a heavy and delicious weight; and we ceased to live long moments. We stopped there as if passed out, submerged in the flow of being, with all our sonorous blood rushing back to our hearts.

Iule said:

- Once I took your hand while you were sleeping. I put it against my throat. I would have liked to die like that.

- I, little Iule, was going to cry in the woods. I don't know why I was crying.

None of us said the word of love. No one had taught us that, but nature had taught us one thing more beautiful than all names and which was love itself. Her nervous young life still quivered when I approached. We kept throwing our lips at each other.

The aromas with the days were more subtle. The wind carried the powerful scent of summer. The earth was of the age of the world's first mornings. The whole forest rustled, quivered with a soul of sap and birds. Every second was a birth, every second together weaved eternity. There were immense trees there, muscular for centuries, and they were rejuvenated with leaves and nests: the blade of grass grown during the night was not younger. The wind and the light also lived. We drank the silence like deep water at the edge of a well. Iule! had you and I lived before this divine time? We were born to each other with the first kiss and with each new kiss we were born again. Our life was like the continuous blossoming of small lentils in a pond.

We thus advanced into the unknown heart of the forest, seeking our food in the trees and on the ground. She leaned on my shoulder, I wrapped my arms around her belt, and I whistled like birds, she sang. Suddenly she let herself fall, with her desire ripe as a fruit, and we did not walk any further. In the evening, I cut down branches; I gathered them on the roof; I spread a litter of leaves. There had come to me a soft tenderness for the ease of her body, a desire to keep her cradled voluptuously in my human strength. When she was tired, I carried her in my arms. I told him:

- If one day you find in this forest a place that you like more than the others, there I will build a house for us.

The valleys gutted the light undulation of the forests. Rock like a bone tore the spongy earth, the ancient humus of giant vegetation. Mossy blocks, deep veins of stone perpetuated a primitive chaos. This new aspect of the universe charmed and terrified our virgin senses. In our ignorance, we imagined that a city had once been built there, attested by ruins. The surf persisted, abrupt, violent, the processes and the vertebrae of the anatomy of a monstrous beast, emerging from the savage ages of the world. Iule with cries ventured; but I was strangely throbbing, seized with an obscure religious feeling. The slopes then became steeper: in a sandstone debacle there was nothing but the silver tremor of the birches. And now I could see that this was one of the shapes of the earth,

The harsh landscape sank again, outlined the indentation of a wild valley, filled with a melting pot of trees and shrubs. Under the scree of rusty tiger rocks, a stream ran, a trickle of clear, cold water which foamed and bubbled in small eddies of gold and emerald. Since we had lived in the forest, we had not experienced such joy. We parted the branches; they curved in the vault as we passed; and bare legs, with the coolness of the wave on our burning skins, we went upstream. Luminous rings circled our ankles and knees, depending on the depth: we were obliged to hold on to the banks so as not to slip on the fatty stones of wrack. And sometimes Iule or I, leaning over the stream, we would draw the wave from it in the palm of our hand and bring it to our lips. It had been so long since our thirsts were appeased only in the small pools of the undergrowth! Fresh blood flowed through us with this water shining like frost. It seemed to us that we were really there at the tabernacle of mystery and solitude, with that little music of silence that gurgled against the stones. She pressed her finger to my mouth and said to me:

- Listen, we only hear the little thing.

And there was, in fact, in this great peace of the heart of the forest, only the dull, continuous noise of our life.

The water slowly clouded over: we saw that evening had come. And that day, we hardly thought of hunger: wild fruits, almonds and pine cones were now enough to feed us. The rich do not know how little man needs to feed himself. She laid her head on my shoulder and we fell asleep by the stream.

The next day I say to Iule:

- If you want, this is where I'll build the house.

So I went into the forest with my ax, having my plan. I choose young trees that are slender and straight. On the first day I chopped two, then I cut them down, and the following days I cut down three more. I divided them in equal parts, I split them, moreover, in the direction of their length, as the woodcutter splits his logs; and at one end of each of these sections as I made the shape of a stake. I cut a large mortise at the other end.

Then halfway up we looked for firm and deep ground. I traced the boundaries of the house so that it was sheltered by the trees on the west side. And then, having dug the earth with the ax, I began to butt the woods by driving them into the trench. A Pali thus arose, the primitive enclosure of men living in the forest. And only, when I was done with this job, I started squaring the roof frame. Iule clapped his hands, for now the ends of the pieces, cut into tenons, were inserted into the hollow of the mortises; and all had a slight inclination for the flow of water. A narrow opening served as an entrance and oriented towards the east. I then filled the joints with fern. Here, with my only ax for tool, I had equaled myself to the naive art of the first builder.

The work was patient and difficult. No sooner had I raised the roof when it collapsed; and weeks perhaps had passed; we had to start over with new courage. But we who had lost track of time did not measure the length of the effort by the shortness of the days. Each brought his task, and without knowing it, we were in our way humble workers of eternity: we had built the house as the ant raises its light domes, as the bee builds its cells. An ancient instinct, coming from far away races, had presided over our industry. I did not yet know that the man is only repeating the gesture that another man naively made before him. In the pride of the accomplished work, I cried under the trees: I did not see that while I was there, combining forms and gravity, a thoughtful ancestor gently came out of the forest and advised me. Iule, come now, spread a bed of fresh ferns for our love. Our peaceful nights will laugh at the downpour and the hurricane. And here is the stream, here is the stone on which, in front of the door, you will light the fire.

I was going on a hunt. I had made a supple and terrible bow; figures engraved with a knife decorated it, and it was very tall. My arrows were reaching for the highest leaves. Iule said:

- Here. You are now the first of men. You are more handsome than the one who, with a big cane and feathers on his head, walked over there in front of the regiment. You built the house and when you go with your arrows, you are terrible.

However, I was still the same Old Man; but love had come and one day we had wounded each other with the point of the knife. And we had drunk our blood. This was Iule's idea. With my blood red on her lips, she cried:

- Now I have your life in me and I gave you mine.

The woods watched this tender and furious little woman, whose mouth kissed as she had bitten.

Every evening, Iule went to pick up cones in the pine forest. Now, once, she suddenly came home, short of breath, and said to me:

- Little Old Man, a man's face was there behind the trees and was looking at me.

I rushed forward, I was armed with the ax. I would have avenged our dear violated solitude at the cost of my life. Shadows stretched and I hadn't seen the dreaded human entered our realm. I came back to the house and said to Iule:

- See, the iron is wet with blood.

She saw that I was kidding: she was no longer as confident as she had actually seen a man.

- I assure you, however, she said, he had a mouth and eyes like you.

- It was a tree, little Iule, nothing but a tree.

My laughter sounded happily under the pale sky.

I didn't like her telling me about Iacq. A jealous leaven still fermented at the idea that this boy had laid his hand on his virgin flesh. It was also a painful regret that he was no longer there to give me tobacco. Yes, I had to smoke dry leaves now: his tobacco had a more delicate taste. I couldn't forget that, I blamed myself for not being able to think of Iacq without both resentment and gratitude. But one day when we were sitting with Iule under the birches among the rocks, we were admiring our roof, she said to me:

- Think then of the face that Iacq would make if he could suspect that you alone with your hands built this house! He wouldn't want to laugh anymore.

Oh ! that day she could talk to me about him as much as she wanted. She thus gave me the pleasure of despising Iacq as a coarse and vain man, like a man whom I had the right to regard with cold eyes from the height of my pride. If only this crazy little Iule hadn't joined him so often behind the door to laugh together at this thing he always said!

- You see, she said, he is beautiful. All the girls love her because of it. But you, you know how to read books and here you have built this house.

So I looked her in the eye.

- Iule, talk to me frankly. Have you never once felt your life stirred in you thinking of him?

And she answered me:

- Once I went into the woods; I rolled on the ground as if I had been stung by a bee. I don't know what would have happened if at this moment he had come.

She made this confession to me so simply that I felt no anger, because since she had given me her love, she no longer lied and once again she had spoken according to nature. Myself, with this fresh life of the first woman close to mine, I had become another younger Little Old Man. It only takes a roof first and everything changes: man is already aware of a destiny. He can say: my house, and by saying so, he thinks of the one that is near him and of the children he will have from her.

Iule with flexible twigs plaited mats. She meshed baskets. I cut from the roots the humble utensils that were used for our meals. A stump became our table. It was, with more experience, the small industry of the early days that we had spent in the forest. And I imagined securing a door made of branches, which closed us in our mystery of love, with supple twisted elbow tree ties. There came sour apples to the branches of the aigrins; we also ate blackberries, sloes and dogwoods. Every day new fruits were revealed to us: under the chestnut trees the ground was strewn with chestnuts from the other autumn; and there were small wild hazelnuts, the red berries of the rose hips, the oily almond of the oak trees; the milky cone of the pine cone abounded. Or else I would go into the forest, cut down living flesh and then Iule, hitting the stone, lit the fire. A hedgehog sometimes, as in the days of the hut, would come up to the house: we were doing him no harm.

We lived innocent and charmed. A sense inclined us towards the mystery, towards the beauty of the sky and the hours, a sensibility filled with wonder of children in front of a prodigy. It was so nice, this Iule plucking the dew from her hair and dripping it rainbow in the cool morning, with dazzled eyes! Lying on her stomach next to me, she watched the streaks of sunlight glide over my skin like ruddy beetles and she screamed with pleasure. She smelled of the rising day, the damp bark, the mist rising from the water, the wind coming from afar with its baskets of aromas. It smelled of ripe wheat and bread. She was for my sweet madness the little flesh with a wild taste which already lived in the womb of all the mothers of her race and which one day had come to me from the depths of time by the way of pain and death. This, little Iule, I wasn't telling you yet; it was an idea which stirred obscurely in me and only elucidated with time. And nevertheless, when with my finger I brushed the golden grain of your shoulders as I spelled out the letters of the old book, she was already sliding to the edge of my thought. O Iule! one thing always derives from another; all of them have their roots in the deep forest of the origins. A child comes out of the city and he sees another child coming to him and they both left at the appointed time: they have not stopped walking towards each other through the duration of the centuries. Your life, dear Iule, has been dedicated to me from all eternity. And now, in this green solitude, soothing our hunger with the fruits of the forest, drinking the sap and the chills of the earth at the springs of the morning, we were the same as the first man and the first woman and we were starting humanity again. However if any of the cities had entered the forest and seen us near the stream with the clear holes in our skin under our rags, he would have denied us a human soul.

So here it is: one day Iule came back once more from the woods quite pale, telling me that she had seen the same face which had appeared to her one evening.

- I assure you, Old Man, it is not an idea. There is another man in the forest. He was there alive like you in front of me. He was looking at me, I dared not make a movement. And then he disappeared as he had come.

I took my ax as the first time and together, talking to each other in low voices, we went under the trees, on the side where she had seen it. I heard the beatings of our hearts in the silence, I only heard that. The man had a gray beard and cunning eyes; Iule affirmed it; and he walked on all fours, he ran like an animal. In her fear, she imagined him terrible. I myself was no longer so sure that the ax would not fall out of my hands if suddenly he stood up behind an oak tree. The ground sank: a rusty puddle, a stagnation of water and stagnant leaves soaked the fold of the ravine. I stood there, breathless: the fresh imprint of a wide footstep sank into the spongy humus. A man had passed there; the strides then crumpled the foam at mid-slope. They got lost in a rubble scree. Loneliness, the mystery closed on this passage of a human being made like us.

Our battles extended over the following days. Paths ran through the woods, narrow, cut by the teeth of rabbits, sometimes made by tall fauns. The forest had no other roads. We slipped away, on the lookout, watching the tracks. Old traces had dried up, footsteps that always sank deeper and then ceased to be visible. Once Iule picked up some freshly picked mushrooms that the man had probably dropped. Then, one morning, the footsteps reappeared at the edge of a flowered area, a starry valley like an August sky, bushy like the mosaic of a garden: someone had come and had cut the stems in large sheaves. And that day, having greatly dilated my nostrils, I thought I smelled a distant delicious aroma in the air and I asked Iule:

- Don't you smell tobacco coming from over there?

- Yes, she said. If it was Iacq!

This idea made me laugh. Why would the boy have come to this forest? He said that no one could ever get out of it, having entered it once. And then, with a strange sweetness, I thought deeply that perhaps another man one day would share with me a scented tobacco like that of Iacq. No, I thought then, let a tree crush him instead, that one! And I hadn't said anything to Iule.

Days passed; the prints were erased; the subtle scent no longer pierced through the acrid green vent of the sap. But as one evening we were sitting in front of the door, eating chestnuts, it suddenly seemed to me that a face was hidden behind the red trunks of the pines.

- Believe me, it is this man, breathed Iule. Tomorrow he will come into this house, if you will let him.

I ran towards the pine forest; he disappeared ; but in the distance someone coughed. I slept that night with the ax between my fists.

There, yes, I could no longer doubt: the forest had an inhabitant. A fierce and devious loner prowled the limits of our domain. Perhaps he had come there before us: he seemed to know the mysterious escapes of the thickets better than we did. O what irony, Iule! We thought we were running away from men forever and there was a man there, with a heart like our heart, living there the free life of the woods. You wept with annoyance; I did not yet dare to tell you what new and profound thing had arisen in me. I thought: what miseries greater than ours drove this man to take refuge in this forest? I was trembling at the thought of knowing that he was more unhappy than us, with a pain that we had ignored. I no longer held a grudge against the unknown human. May he share the forest with us, Little by little it ended up seeming natural to me, since we too had come there, driven out by our hatred of men. I did not know that deep in the most distressed hearts still remains the ancient fraternal bond. I had fled the tribes and my solidarity was already awakening, yearning for this sad passerby of loneliness. It was a feeling I would not have known in the bloody melee of the cities. It made my heart swell; my heart rose to my lips one day. I say to Iule: It was a feeling I would not have known in the bloody melee of the cities. It made my heart swell; my heart rose to my lips one day. I say to Iule: It was a feeling I would not have known in the bloody melee of the cities. It made my heart swell; my heart rose to my lips one day. I say to Iule:

- See, however, if this one had neither wife nor child! You have me like I have you. Perhaps he suffers from being alone, he who had already suffered among men.

She answered me precisely:

- Formerly, Old Man, you would have gone to meet him with the ax. You wouldn't have thought so far.

A bitter jay quarrel cried out in the trees. We saw the feathers fly under the pecks they were tearing.

"The jay was there alone too," I said, and then a second came. Now it's up to who will kill the other. Believe me, man is not made to look like beasts.

The old almanac once again pounded in my chest. He quivered with warm humanity as if all the hearts of men were throbbing in his tender apologues.

- Well, said Iule, you are the master of following your idea.

Suns still ran and the traces of the man seemed to have been definitely lost in the vast solitude. There was only the silence of the trees on the furtive wake of this life of a creature. And I thought I felt I was going to miss something. A still elementary soul cannot be explained: it has movements that it ignores and which already are the high life of beings. When the bricklayers and lumberjacks came, I had only thought of bread. These lived together, they were not unhappy. This wandering brother of the woods, with his lonely ailment, was much more of my family.

"He saw your ax, he will have trembled," said Iule.

I shook my head.

- No, it is not that. A man does not fear another man.

Now I no longer left with the ax. If the man had reappeared, I would have screamed at him, I would have shown him my unarmed hands.

Once, having followed the course of the water, we were suddenly very far from the house; we had left in the morning, with the desire to go how far this water would go. Sometimes she was encased between high sections of rocks: we would then go down to her bed, wet to the waist. There we tasted a little charmed horror; and then the walls were lowered; the procession ended in slowly flattened waves. We resumed our journey along the shore, under the green arches. The air was heavy and milky; a light mist misted the thickets; the big flies slept, glued to the leaves. And then around noon the sky was torn apart, a fine shower of sunlight gilded the vapors which rose; the forest smoked in the ruddy heat.

I went in front of Iule, clearing a passage for him between the branches. But soon fatigue overwhelmed him; she wanted to rest near the stream, and hardly had she stretched out, her eyes closed, she fell asleep. I continued to walk alone for a little while. I was no longer thinking of the man, I was listening to the forest waking up in the clear light. Its enormous life intoxicated me, the smell of saffron and tannin effluent from the warm bark, the infinite rustling of arterioles belatedly resusing the humidities of the night in the sun. I, too, with the sonorous hum of blood at my temples, was a part of this life. And I walked slowly, watching the leaves move, an insect running, trembling in the woods a silence of clarity.

The trees thinned; I remained seized, my heart in my hands, seeing there suddenly, under the bare sky, the man sitting near a strange shelter and sorting the grass. The site was savage and delicious, boulders of rock, a small forest of foxgloves, seneçons, doradillas, a savagery of nature rolling in large, variegated waves in the indentation of a clearing. A blanket of ivy covered the walls of the house. It was a car without wheels sunk askew in the ground, one of those fairground maringotes like they came to carousels at suburban festivals. And I couldn't see the eyes of the man; he had a long gray beard that ran down to his chest.

I would not have believed that the sight of a creature would have given me so much pleasure. I dared not go forward for fear he would see me. I held the branches apart with my hands and I stood there without breathing. What I was thinking exactly right now, I couldn't have said. It was undoubtedly a confused thing like all the perceptions of my still virgin sensibility and yet it seems to me today that it could have been explained thus: a man and I had come from two opposite points of the world to join us. One day. The almanac did not say anything about it, but a great light was in me which enlightened the Life before me. One thing after one thing had come and all had come in due time: no movement of our will had been necessary to arouse them. Iule and I had simply obeyed the gesture of a hand which had led us towards each other and then led the men towards us. An admirable order thus had presided over each of our steps in the paths of the world. We followed our life: it did not follow us; and no one has taught the stream to seek its level, or the thistle to card its tow, or the squirrel to climb trees. However, we have never seen the water go up its slope nor any earthly thing to oppose the law which was originally assigned to it. When my enlarged temples had taken measure of the effort of my thought, it was this little source of truth which receded its walls like a light trickle of water is enough to clear in the long run the bed where the torrent will pass. We never stopped entrusting ourselves to life:

I stayed a little while looking at the man and the house; and then, as each beat of my heart was prolonged in Iule's heart, with stifling steps I went to wake her.

- Hush! don't say anything and get up.

She then came with me and now in her turn she was there, silent, at the treeline, with her eyebrows high. A mystery gently enveloped this life of a defenseless man who confidently abandoned himself to the care of nature. Nothing in the world was more tender and more beautiful than flowered peace, the throbbing of silence around the quiet solitary, as if invisible providences were circling and watching over his reverie. He was still sitting on the threshold: he had finished sorting the herbs and he was standing still, his hands on his knees. With his forehead facing the sky, he seemed to be contemplating the beauty of the day. The beard had eaten his face up to the eyebrows; her hair fell over her shoulders like the foliage of an oak; he had clear child's eyes.

Doubtless life in the forest had stolen his senses; he sensed an unusual presence, held out his big hairy head.

"Talk to him," Iule whispered to me.

But what would I have said to this man, me, such a young boy? I only wanted to stroke her long hair like a son.

- You see, Iule, it is better that it is you.

So boldly she took a step, coughed and the old man was now looking at us with irritated eyes.

- Who are you ? Do not enter here! Go away ! he cried.

He spoke as if the forest had belonged to him. I had taken Iule's hand and we dared neither move forward nor backward. We did not know what to answer him, suddenly emerged from the green shadows, with our fearful faces in the high light. He stood up, walked violently across the clearing. I regretted not having taken the ax, but Iule had already fallen to her knees and was saying:

- Dad ! don't hurt us.

No one had taught her this movement, and she was saying something tender and filial there, rising from the depths of her life. The man stopped, ran a hand over his large face.

"No one other than you called me by that name," he said.

And he was looking at us now without anger. His beard waved in the wind of the words he said to himself:

- They are the little ones of the forest. At their age! What the hell did they do to other men?

He rested his hand on my shoulder.

- Tell me where you come from.

- From there, I don't know.

I had answered thus to the bricklayers.

Iule laughed.

"This one doesn't like to talk," she said. But there. Once there was a tree in the countryside, near the city. He came to the tree just as I was coming too. We had never seen each other. We shared a piece of bread together. And then he took me by the hand, we never left each other. This is how we arrived in this forest.

Now I was laughing too, hearing him speak as if there really had been only that in our life.

However, she was closer to the truth than if she had described in detail the daily adventure of our famines and our caravans. Life is limited to a few essential lines and a small wave of a great river is enough to give the banks the taste of salt or honey. But the old man, seeing us both laughing, began to distrust. The loneliness had not yet expressed all the bitterness of his old wounds.

- Who assures me, he said, that this is the truth?

And he was sad, a cloud isolated him from us. I raised my straight eyes, I said frankly:

- She said what is. Little Old Man never cheated on anyone. Once he almost killed with his ax a man who had deceived him and then he gave him life.

- Iacq, yes! cried Iule.

There you are, I was talking like a little savage of the woods whose ideas have no follow-up and whirl with a wandering flight of leaves in the autumn wind. We often said, Iule and I, things understood by us alone in the simple unity of our life like a great path in the forest.

The man was small, fearful, quick in his tracks, like any creature who has unlearned concealment in trees. He put his hand on my shoulder, buried his clear pupils in my temples, thus drinking my sincerity from its source. The minute was solemn, our lives one in front of the other swayed in suspense. And finally gently he said:

- So there are people who do not lie! Welcome to my poor cabin, you who have clear eyes like daylight.

He led us to the green house. Twists of ivy hung across the threshold: only in winter did he pull the door open; and night and day entered freely. Almost ten years ago, having come to the forest, he had found this abandoned trailer there. Perhaps its inhabitants were dead: he had never known how she had gotten to this wild place, far from the roads. The brambles and nettles had already covered it: it had lost its wheels, all empty like the carcass of a boat after a shipwreck. And now we were in this old thing of life as the very heart of the old man's destiny. With trees blown down by the wind he made a table, a notebook, a narrow frame which he filled with ferns and which served as a berth. Shelves supported the utensils necessary for his meals. A skylight with panes meshed with cobwebs shed a green light on bundles of dry grass hanging from the partitions. There was also, hung above the bed, in a copper border, a small portrait of a woman and an old calendar crossed out. Why, seeing that Iule was looking at the portrait, he cried suddenly with anger:

- Close your eyes: there is blood on it.

He took the portrait and threw it under the ferns. His hands were shaking: he was lost in an idea for a little while, forgetting our presence. And then he tells us:

- A poor man like me has a long life behind him and every hour is not good. The rain, the snow and the wind have not erased anything.

He appeared to me concentrated and fierce, with the sad evil of an unknown thing buried in his days. I dared not question him, feeling the heavy weight of pain on him. He went to the threshold, inhaled the air strongly and then came back to offer us some honey and bread which he broke with a hammer and soaked in water.

- Every month, he said, I go to the Convent of the Fathers, six leagues walk from here. I know the dates from the calendar. The moons and months are marked there. I imagine that nothing has changed since the time when he regulated the hours of my life. And, after all, a day is only a day in the span of time. I bring herbs to the good Fathers which they distill and in exchange they give me bread, salt, a little elixir and the fruits that do not ripen in the forest. I don't need more to live.

His words often remained mysterious to me. He spoke less simply than good man Jean. Sometimes he seemed to be talking to himself in a low voice. You, dear Iule, you paid less attention to what he said than to the foods he put on the table. The bread may be moldy, but it's still bread: you were a little embarrassed to eat it with a spoon, until then you had only used your teeth and your fingers. My God ! that once again the taste for it had passed away! He seemed to take pleasure in studying the frankness of our sensations on our faces. I could not suppress a savage laughter when, having crumpled tinder-colored leaves between his thumb and forefinger, he gave me my share, saying that it was tobacco he had planted near the hut. If someone had come up against our hut, we could only have given him the bitter fruits of the forest. His poverty was rich alongside our destitution.

- Father, said Iule to him, by what name must we call you from afar if, coming towards you, we find the house empty?

His eyes seemed to question the little portrait under the ferns and he remained silent for a moment. Finally, moving his hairy forehead, he replied:

- I'm the one who no longer has a name. But it will be very sweet to me that you continue to call me Father.

"I used to be Frilotte," she said. Now they call me Iule.

- Frilotte… Little Old Man…

He laughed softly.

- You and he, however, had a father, a mother.

Iule shrugged his shoulders.

- There, they all asked us the same thing. My father, maybe his neck was cut off. As for my mother, she probably drank and chatted with men like Mama. Little Old Man, very little, slept under the bridges. We don't know anything else.

The old man's eyelids fluttered; his gaze grew wet. No tear had yet cried over our childhood. And now he was holding our heads together in his broad palms and stroking us.

- Little ... little ... O misery!

We were there tenderly before his great life as children. We were warm to his heartbeat. He looked at a point in the sky, seemed to question someone in space. A weak breath breathed out in his beard.

- Why does such a thing have to be?

I could not have found a word; but Iule, closer to nature, had a delicious impulse.

"We didn't mean to hurt you," she said.

He dried his eyes with his finger and smiled, saying:

- You who have not despaired of life, you are higher before her than I, the old tree. Hearts of good courage, I thought I had nothing more to learn and you bring me the right lesson.

We only half understood what he meant and yet we were stirred by something deep within us, as if our race and all those of old humanity were throbbing in the long grief of this man. Iule began to play with his beard and said:

- You are not happy, Father.

"I try to forget the harm that men have done to me and the one that I have done to them myself," he replied, shaking his head.

Communion spread, the fraternal warmth on the humble family united in the heart of life by such a destiny. A huge oak tree above us was buzzing with flies and bees. We were together under its arches like a small humanity detached from the big one and which feels the old fibers pushing back. And the man and the tree made the same deep shadow. He told us that one day he had heard the shock of the ax; it was the time when I started to build the house; the whole forest had bled from its own anguish; and then, moving at the noise, he had come, he had seen two human beings prowling in the outraged silence of the solitudes. That day he had left for the cabin, sobbing like a child. He who for ever believed to have fled men, he found them in the forest he had chosen to die there an unknown death, returned to nature. And then again an invincible sympathy had drawn him. Once he had called us: no one having answered, he had slipped under the roof, he had seen the bed, the mats, our young industries.

- O Little Old Man, cried Iule, a man has seen the bed!

Why was she talking to me like that, she who hadn't hidden her legs for Iacq? I did not understand immediately that the bed was also part of his nakedness and that modesty had come to him with love. The fibers of man quiver with desire and heroism and after love he goes to fight, to hunt, leaving the woman at home, the faithful guardian of nuptial and secret matters.

The old man smiled and replied:

- Your bed was then for me the bed of an enemy. Now that you have called me by my father's name, it will be a girl's bed.

The silence rustled as light as a May rain. Iule shamelessly pulled me by the head and kissed me on the mouth.

He took us to see his bees. By the time it was right, he had captured the swarm from a great distance and carried it near a hollow tree trunk, on the edge of an expanse of heather. Ancient men had cut down the pines that once grew there. A vast wasteland now unfolded, an ashy earth clumped with purple tufts with a sweetly bitter aroma. The bees had chosen the tree to build the hive there; but over time they had swarmed in their turn. From the primitive city other cities had emerged which also had settled in the vicinity of the heather. Together they gave him honey and wax in abundance: he kept only the honey, he took the wax to the convent of the Fathers. They knew their master: he walked to the threshold of the hive and none hurt him. Their flight grazed it and then fell back to the edge of the opening or scattered over the flower gardens of the wasteland. A long ruddy shiver vibrated in the air, a golden wind like summer at the gates of a city. In multitudes, from the flow of a river they entered, left, snored. Around his great forehead, they seemed to be the whirlwind of his thoughts. And we were there, I mute and trembling, Iule uttering little cries, both shaken by an interior joy in front of this image of life. Around his great forehead, they seemed to be the whirlwind of his thoughts. And we were there, I mute and trembling, Iule uttering little cries, both shaken by an interior joy in front of this image of life. Around his great forehead, they seemed to be the whirlwind of his thoughts. And we were there, I mute and trembling, Iule uttering little cries, both shaken by an interior joy in front of this image of life.

We knew the rabbit lodge, the mole galleries, the maze of anthills; we were still ignorant of the bee house, the fair porches, the miracle of the juices of the earth turned into fragrant cakes. A people infinitely working behind the partitions, distilling the essences, doing there little times a thing of eternity. And I was seized with respect as in front of a mystery, a force greater than that which was in me. The whole forest rustled with a subtle flight of spirits, while the old man explained the cells, the males and the queens, the laying of eggs, the drama of love and death from which the buzzing hive was endlessly reborn. Iule then had the child's naive question:

- Tell us, father, who told them all this?

There it was, it was the same thing she and I said in front of the stream, the tree, the fruit and the dawn. She kept coming back to us and no one had answered us yet. Our souls in us tormented like a blind man in a house without doors. We didn't know that same question, men of ages had asked before us; and to these neither the water nor the wind nor the other wonders of the world had answered.

The old man simply said:

- Life perhaps, the life which to yourselves, little ones, taught you to feed yourselves on the fruits of the forest and to protect yourself from the rain by building a roof for yourself.

The little bird that makes its nest with blades of grass too would have said that, if he could have spoken. Life infinitely comes out of life and everything was already in substance at its origins. I think so now, after having dwelt for a long time on the obscure mystery. But then it was still a new thing that a human mouth expressed this conjecture. I did not know that I, who had done a work of life by building the house, was myself a part of life over time.

The day fell, a coolness rose from the depths. It was the old man who warned us of the hour: we would have stayed until nightfall looking at the beehive. He showered us with honey and walking in front of us, he made us follow a path that he himself had made and which shortened the distance between his roof and ours. The forest was now populated by the steps that for years he had placed one in front of the other, ending up being the everywhere visible soul of the thickets. Other paths crossed the one which twisted towards our hut; and hardly did they trace a slight wrinkle in the great mysterious life of the silve. We who lived near the stream would have ignored them for a long time.

The wind had risen with the full moon, a clear and limpid wind like the sound of water. It seemed to flow from among the trees, to stretch out with pools of dormant light on the mosses and ferns. A blue mist drowned the clearings: we could not see the entire moon in the heavy mass of the peaks. It slipped between the leaves, filtered in slow drops like streams of milk. A pallor of dead light trailed in the cold transparencies of the shadows. The moonlit night entered the house with us. I said to Iule:

- Life ! Life ! O Iule! Think about it!

She had been silent part of the way, harboring a secret urge in her wild heart; and now she was loosening her teeth and following her idea without answering me.

- You see, Old Man, it is not fair that a man alone has so many beehives. If you believe me, one day when he is in the forest, you will carry a swarm.

- That, no, neither now nor ever. You and I gave him the name of Father.

She jumped on my neck and cried with a fury of love:

- You alone, Old Man, are all men to me. There is neither father nor brother for Iule.

She expressed there a feeling according to the very heart of life and once she had already said it, at the time of our visit to the bricklayers. All her life, the woman gives it all at once to the one who happened to her first and then the other men can come or go their way: her love has bled only once. If I had said: "I will leave in the morning, I will strike this man whom you first called father and who has bees between the temples," she herself would have passed me the ax. I wouldn't have loved her less for that.

We returned to see the old man. Twice the earth had turned and that day the rain was falling gently. I had killed a squirrel near the house. I imagined the joy of the lonely when I said to him:

- He was all fresh of life. See, I killed him for you.

But as soon as he saw the blood, he pushed my hand away and said harshly:

- You sacrificed living flesh. Now your hand will be red forever. How do you want that between you and me, there is not the thought of this death?

And then he looked at the squirrel.

- It was the gaiety of the forest. His female will look for him in the shadows and will not find him any more. Maybe he had little ones.

Iule laughed.

- It's just a beast and you talk about it as if it were one of us.

- Life is life! he cried, shaking his hairy forehead. There is no more life in Little Old Man and you than there was in this animal. And everything that lives is sacred. It only took one gesture to take his life away; and no force in the world could restore it to him. However, he had a heart and lungs and flesh like you two. He had a fierce and tender little soul that cried out with pleasure and pain.

Iule stopped laughing and she looked at the squirrel with astonished eyes. His breath was running fast. She hugged me.

- Look! If this beast had really had a heart as he says! Neither you nor I would have thought of that.

I too kept my gaze fixed on this poor thing of life stiffened on the ground. I no longer felt the old pride of the man who slaughtered a prey. I thought, "There, he's right. I killed her and I couldn't bring her back to life. I couldn't have said why I was hiding my hands behind my back.

He saw me sad and thoughtful. His face lit up; he had the mobile and fresh sensations of the young men of humanity.

- I read your eyes, he said happily. Now this dead beast will quiver in you every time the bad temptation comes back to you. You will no longer strike any living animal, having received the measure of life yourself. See, however: if you and I had eaten of his flesh, we would not have done anything else than if we had eaten of each other since life is the same in all beings. Formerly, when I lived with men, I did not feel repugnance to eat meat: all did so by a savage instinct. And then one day, having come with my gun into this forest, I killed a wood pigeon. My hunger was ardent: I devoured it still hot, in the last thrill of life; I tore its fibers with red teeth, like a carnivorous beast. But suddenly the taste of fresh blood made my heart turn. I looked deep inside and was horrified. Believe me, it will be the same for you if you want to listen to nature.

He bent down, piously took the squirrel in his hands, and showing me the spade, he told me to go ahead, outside the confines of the enclosure. That's what he called the corner of the forest where he lived.

'Death hasn't entered here yet,' he said, 'but go over there to the thicket and dig a little pit.

I did as he said and the beast now rested in the light earth. The damp foliage wept over his pacified spirits. And we stayed there a little while without speaking. Then the white beard trembled.

- If one day, coming through the forest, you find me lying lifeless on the threshold, don't wake me. I want to sleep near my bees. Time will take care of the rest. It is sweet to me to think that the sun and the rain will soon consume my bones. And from the life that there was in me, flowers and foliage will be born where the rumor of beehives will continue to hum endlessly.

He spoke with serenity about death: he did not want it and he waited for it. But we, with our young life force, were moved at the idea that we would have to see this man lying stiff on the ground. A shadow hovered; the sources of sensibility quivered. And Iule was holding me in her arms, crying.

- Will you also, Little Old Man, die one day? What will become of me after you close your eyes? Please don't ever hurt me.

The old man shrugged his shoulders:

- Think what you want, you who have a manly heart. They all said the same thing. And then someone comes and drinks the tears on their mouth.

The veins of his forehead twitched: he blew angrily into his beard; and he was looking out of the forest. And then, pressing his chest with his hands, he cried out, his mouth gaping, like a barking beast:

- Old suffering! Won't you ever shut up?

Iule put his finger to his forehead and whispered in my ear:

- Mama also sometimes like a madwoman shouted against the men ...

He saw us, remained seized as if he had spoken in a moment of bewilderment and with a gesture of the hand in front of his eyes, he seemed to chase away a painful vision.

- Children... children. Is it you who are there? Come closer, defend me against myself. I am such a poor man.

He gently stroked Iule.

- You see, it is not true, you, you are not like the girls of the cities. These lie with painted mouths; and then there is a man who does a bad thing and goes to atone for his fault in a forest. Do not try to understand: this is a story that only I still remember.

The disastrous images dispersed. He pulled our hands into his and now he closed his eyes, he seemed to be talking to himself.

- These are innocent and free life. They have the charmed age of the mornings of the world. What can they have in common between them and me?

He made us enter the house and as the first time gave us fruit and bread. He tells us about his life in the forest: he only began to live the day he separated from the men. When he returned from bringing his herbs to the Fathers, a warmth of humanity remained in him and was enough to fill his solitude. However, the god they worshiped was not his; but they were benevolent and prayed for his salvation. And winters had followed summers; his body had become accustomed to inclement weather. Morning and evening, he went down to bathe in the stream. He himself, with the clothes and tools passed to him by the monks, had made his clothes and his working tools. His evenings, in the time of long nights, were lit with resin torches: by their light he dreamed or read old books. He knew the essences of the forest: all were beautiful, being life; and each had its special virtues. Fruits were also familiar to him: he knew their properties; a small number harbored poisons. And even the most defiant of birds do not fear a man if he is free from wickedness. From the threshold he whistled: magpies descended to the tips of the branches and then with small hops advanced towards the house.

Iule suddenly shouted:

- Little Old Man can read books too!

She had put her hand on my head and was looking me in the eye proudly. But I felt so humble near this man of great life who knew the secrets! I bowed my head.

- There, yes. Once an old man like you taught me to read the book.

I spoke of it like a Bible. How could I have suspected that a poor thing of the ages like this, written for ploughmen, was just an irrelevant leaflet in the great inexhaustible sap of the tree of human knowledge?

- Do you have it there? he said.

I pulled it from my chest. For a little while, I wore it rolled up in a piece of Iule's beautiful dress. The dress had worn out: it was nothing but a rag on her shoulders; all of her flesh was going through and she and I were going almost naked into the forest. But a poor shred still contains enough wealth to make charity from a cover to a book that goes away from having been handled too much. Iule had cut a piece in the fabric and she had protected the twisted fibers of the paper. She would not have done otherwise for a talisman, for the sacred ashes of an ancestor of her race.

He was moved, now holding the open book in his hands. His nostrils fluttered: he looked at me with a strange tenderness.

- Oh ! he said, you know more than me if you have grasped all the beauty that is hidden here. There is more real wisdom in a little book like this than in all the books on earth. Never read another one. That one surely was a saint who gave it to you.

The rainy air cleared: a light air rushed in, a warm, blond light that smoked on the leaves. All the herbs sparkled with jewels. The arteries of the soil, soaked deeply, drank the waters. The forest dripped, sang in the rustle of fountains. We went to see the bees again: they climbed in the heat, drunk with the sun after the rain, their wings quivering. He showed us how they made honey, their brushes fluffed with pollen, the baskets they have on their feet and which they use to collect their harvest. Seeing thus the agile workers hurry, my thoughts returned to themselves. The parable, which sprang from a point of the conjecture, ended in the stammering of the young man drunk with the unknown.

- If life taught them what they are doing there, who taught them life?

My question rose fiery, worried, as if suddenly someone had shouted inside me, in the mystery. He, his forehead bent, gazed at his shadow on the ground.

- If you ask me why this shadow is there, I will turn to the sun: but I cannot tell you which hands threw this sun through space or if it did not exist before all the hands. No man has ever known it and all speak of a god who was at the origin of things. I too, as a child, I stammered his name, trembling. Now I no longer separate him from life: she was always with him. I adore them together across the beauty of the world. Don't ask me any more.

My eyes followed the gesture of his hand towards the shadow and then lost themselves in the orb of which he marked the curve of the sun. I was like the first man before miracles. The abyss in a furrow of fires opened, closed again and I remained on the edge of great darkness, mute, seized with vertigo. What could a wild child like me have understood from these great sublime images? If he had simply evoked the terrible god of the Bible, I would have been terrified, feeling between him and me a dreary impassable barrier. A heavy weight weighed on my temples.

"I don't know what you mean," I stammered.

He stroked my forehead and slowly, like lost in a dream, he spoke.

- Open your eyes and you will see, you who appear a virgin before the mystery. The obscure still is full of light if one approaches it with an ingenuous soul. The key is to know nothing. He alone understands who has learned nothing and looks at nature with fresh eyes. So do not listen to what I say to you: I am an old man who has groped for the light, while you, not having known a lie, you hold the truth in the palm of your hand. I envy your young soul which has nothing to forget. Open your eyes, springing from your own strength towards the obvious. Believe without reasoning with the astonished faith of life before life. You will hear the true eternal god answer you from the bottom of things. It is in the sprig of moss as well as in the oak and throughout the forest. He is in thunder and he is in the light sound of the wind. It is he who beats in the beating of your heart and he spins with your shadow at your feet. When Iule kisses you on the mouth, it is between your lips. Look for him everywhere in your life and at the limits of your life; you will still find it in what men call death and which is only the beginning of life.

I was shaken by an inner force. I was thinking :

- Perhaps this one too is a god.

And there he was, in a great light, like the apostles, like the saints, like those who with raised hands walk before other men. Ideas are seeds that fall to the ground and do not germinate immediately; and one day they break the hard rock and the whole field is up. When later, having matured them, I was able to relate them to all things, the world divinely lit up before me. But then I still only saw the tree, the blade of grass, the stream where you had to see the whole universe. Life entered into my being like water filtering from a small spring and now it fills my cisterns.

The old man once again gave us a honey cake: he shared with us what remained of his bread. And as we both returned with our hands entwined by the forest, I said to Iule:

"Didn't you think you sometimes heard the good Maitre Jean speak?"

- Yes, she said. But he always spoke to us about a god who had died on the cross. I don't know his name anymore.

"That one," I said, "was a sad god.

She was hungry and thirsty for love and took my mouth between her lips. A sweet madness passed through my blood: I fell into the leaves with her. I kept telling him:

- O Iule! think about it, you are life!

It was that day that for the first time she put her hand to her side. She was very pale, her eyes faded, and she was moaning softly:

- Something has come, Old Man.

There, the child had cried inside her. I carried her in my arms to the cabin; and then she laughed herself like a little child who doesn't know why she is laughing. O Iule! little Iule, loved with joined hands! you who had come to me from the end of the world to bring me your life, now you had received the Holy Visitation and another life, made up of both of us, was throbbing in your bosom. But none of us suspected that your pain was life knocking on the door. If someone had said: It's the child! we would have looked at each other without understanding.

The thrush hung from the ripe sorbs in the purple forest. We thus knew that it was autumn. There were graceful and cool days, in a fiery must of sap. I always went in front of me, saying like a prayer that is spelled out:

- Life ! O Life! O Life! O Life!

I raised my hand towards the sun; a ruddy wave ran around the edges, the diaphanous and heavy heat of my blood. Life ! O Iule! Life ! I took Iule's hair, I stretched it lengthwise at the tips of my fingers; each was like a fiber of his life, like a little living thing in the sonorous course of his life. I had a sacred joy in looking at the fine trees of the veins on her skin: they resembled the twigs of a leaf, the delicate network of fruit flesh. I had done it this way in the old days and then I didn't know what life was. You first need only the small opening through which a little water springs from the earth and then passes the whole river. My temples were buzzing like a beehive in which bees are captive. I was shouting: Life! Life ! having no other word to say.

The father arrived by the path of the trees. He was sitting at our doorstep by the stream. He drew on his pipe, shook his head between his shoulders, remained silent for a long time, like a man who was already on his way before daybreak. The silence did not weigh on us: we too, for whole days, exchanged only the necessary words. She had her little animal cry, in joy and surprise. Wow ! Wow ! I whistled, with the piaulis of the wind light in my ears like a flute. I had become adept at imitating the song of the new birds that each season brought. We didn't feel the need to say anything to each other in order to understand each other.

When he spoke he said beautiful things. With the trembling of his white beard, he was like an old cherry blossom tree. He seemed to be talking to himself in a low voice.

- Yes, he said, it's the truth. The roof and the tools must be taken from oneself, the house must be an act of will and love. Your wild house, little ones, is more beautiful than the palaces of the cities, having been made to measure your life. One day men will understand this. Everyone on the edge of the woods will have their home and their field according to their dreams.

He always seemed to be looking towards the depths of the forest and he was saying:

- The times will come.

We didn't know what times he wanted to talk about.

He revealed to us the roots, the mushrooms and the herbs; the whole rich man's table grows wild in the forest. We used to cook our harvest or eat it raw, all scented with the smell of the earth. It was also the time of the last fruits: the apple of the rose hips and the barberry, the medlar and the dogwood were never lacking. Nature filled us like a granary of abundance. And once he began to tell us about the earth, the moon and the sun. In the city everyone said: the sun rises and sets. The old almanac on this was in the opinion of most people. We like the others, watching its red disc plunge down to the sky, we thought it was disappearing every evening. And There you go ; now it was revealed to us that the earth alone sank into space.

The universe expanded: our humble lives gasped in vertigo. Yes, that was a great miracle. One step we took after another each time pushed the boundaries of the world. Wasn't that alone, turning on one's feet as the earth turned, already a wonderful thing? We never ceased to be amazed about ourselves and what surrounded us.

Great winds whirled like red millstones; the whole forest was bare. We lit wood fires in front of the hut. I had plugged the joints of the partitions with dry fern.

- You see, said Iule, if only he let you kill the animals, we would have skins that would warm us.

The poor men of old, in their naive industry, had pulled the tow from the woody fibers to clothe themselves with it or had made coats for themselves from the dry leaves. But we, we, were the rejects of the old rotten stumps: perhaps our unknown fathers had slept in good soft sheets. Iule tenderly drew my head to her chest and I, at the heart of her life, between her two folded arms, I was hot as in summer days. Now, too, she sometimes lifted her thick, injured breasts up to my hands. It was a great weight that pulled her body forward like a tree bends under the fruit. She said :

- When you carry them like this with me, I suffer less.

She was trailing a dull, continuous illness; sometimes, like an overcast fruit, she would fall to the ground moaning and shouting:

- Little old man, I think I'm going to die.

It was already the end of winter: little snows had fallen as if with our hands we had shaken flowering apple trees. We had never slept so much; we slept a long dream of forgetfulness and rest. And one by one the little hands of the leaves unfolded in the gentle wind. The grass sprang up with anemones, like drops of milk fallen from the udders of the night. We knew it was spring once again.

I walked through the forest. I went in front of me to the old man's house and said:

- Father, Iule suffers from an illness that we do not know. Don't you have a herb that can help her?

He laughed :

- It's life, kid, it's life.

I was there sad and tilting my head.

- Why then don't you teach us to fear life?

He breathed on my forehead and said:

- Open your eyes and you will understand.

With a great shake deep in my bones, I looked at him.

- Father, has the time come?

A great light was on me and I had the soft heart of a man who was struck on the way. He held me tight in his arms for a little while, with fatherly pressure, and he himself could no longer speak. And finally his beard stirred:

"It's because of the child," he said.

A child ! a little child! Iule's little child! All my life was dead, passed in a cry of delicious agony. We were both crying. And then, holding the heavy weight of my heart in my hands, I ran back through the forest.

I was shouting from afar:

- Iule! Iule!

She came to the threshold and I fell on my knees, still calling her by her dear name without daring to tell her that the child was there. As she was standing, she lifted my head towards her and quite pale, she questioned me, entering her eyes far into mine. His rapid breath ran like the morning wind. She no longer had the same face; it had rather the face of the little Iule who came the first day with me in the forest. She looked like a child Iule and also like someone else who was not yet known to me. There, she already had a little in her hazy eyes of the life of the child she was carrying. Slowly, trembling, she pressed one hand to her side and the other, she held it open under her throat, where her heart was beating strongly. The whole forest fell silent, and with a voice rising from the young sources of his being,

- Do not be mad. I believe it is a small thing of life.

She let herself slide down beside me on the ground; she kissed me tenderly as if to console me. She would not have done it otherwise if she had been unfaithful to me; and she no longer spoke to me. Her mouth tickled me with light warm kisses on the back of my neck. And I, with joy, sobbed between his knees. So I had come running like a messenger of annunciation; and it was she who, warned by nature, suddenly spoke to me about the child while I still held my teeth closed on the divine secret.

Spring came on. Now like the Old Man, she always turned to one side of the forest and she looked ahead. A woman thus in the houses keeps her eyes fixed on the door through which the one who is expected must come. She laughed when she saw the shadow that the curve of her stomach made on the ground. She had the mobile humor, the sly and irritated graces of young animals at the time of the teeth. Sometimes she cried, saying:

- What will we do with the child when he comes? Think a little; in the city they all have dolls that they dress and cradle in their arms. It slowly gets them used to having babies. I have never had a doll. Mama once gave me a silk scarf that she no longer wore. She lived near an old cemetery, an old cemetery where a man always turned the earth. With each stroke of the spade, it was bones that came. See if there is nothing to laugh about! I picked up one of these bones, sewed it into the kerchief and kissed it like a real doll. Believe me, it would be best to put your finger in the child's mouth. You would go dig a little pit.

The wind then turned; she was seized with madness at the idea of having him naked between her little breasts. With the sway of her hips, she imitated the cradle that invites sleep. Once she said:

- It is to die for joy when they start calling you with their little mouths like a strawberry.

However, one day, feeling her breasts tighten, she moaned and put her hand to their swollen ends. And the milk had risen: a clear drop quivered in his fingers and rolled heavily on the grass. Seeing her life thus flow, I said to her:

- Please give me a little, since the little one hasn't come yet.

She squeezed the pink tips gravely and I, who had never known a mother's milk, drank love's milk for the first time in my manhood. He tasted sour and sweet: I wanted to be his little child.

I was now going through the forest without her. I helped the Old Man to collect plants; the monks distilled the juices for dictames and eye drops. He taught me their virtues, most of them were known to him by name. Together we also harvested strawberries and bilberries for Iule. She liked to eat the young nettle and the dandelion. I beat stones and boiled them in jars. These, I had kneaded with loam and then dried in the fire. There was in the almanac a story of a shipwrecked man lost in an uninhabited island and who gradually became a skilled potter. I had read it a hundred times; it corresponded to our life. Each leaf of the old book thus was a lesson. I had only spelled half of it yet: it seemed to me that I would never manage to read it to the last page. The Old Man laughed, always said:

- Believe me, the shoemaker was right. There is more wisdom there than in all the books we have in the city.

After all, we lacked nothing in our destitution. We had a cabin, a table, a bed; the stream never dried up; the earth provided us with herbs and fruits in abundance. When the old friend returned from the convent, he shared the bread with us. He and we, in this fraternal life, were like a family escaped from a disaster, like a small tribe which found itself after distant caravans. Here we are, we looked like this shipwrecked man who had ended up making his own town on the lonely island.

Once, being two to pick herbs near the stream, I said to him:

- Father, the child wants to go out and we do not yet know what name to give him. A tree is called a tree, but a child needs a name like she is Iule and I the Little Old Man. If you wanted to tell us what name we gave you in men, we would call it after you.

He held in his hand a small shovel shaped like a trowel with which he gently lifted the roots. He planted it in the ground, got up, first answered me harshly:

- There used to be a man there who had a face like other men. This one, we called him ...

He let himself fall, wiped his forehead boiling with sweat; and a fiery breath issued from his nostrils.

- Don't ask me that, he said, I told you, I'm the one who no longer has a name.

"Iule would have liked it," I said softly.

Then a cloud clouded his eyes and he was crying tearlessly, his head bowed, looking far into himself.

- Good, that's good. There, yes, it's good that you ask me that, he said finally.

And suddenly his voice dropped, as if he was ashamed to remember his name.

- My name is Jean. Now do as you wish.

I would not have been more moved if at that moment the old master had come out of the woods, saying: "He and I are the same man. My teeth were chattering.

- See, I cried, the other was also called Jean.

The almanac was beating on my heart; it was one of the good times of my life. I returned to Iule and I said to him:

- There will be twice John, because there you are, the Father has the same name as the old master. Isn't that a happy thing?

- Well ! she laughed, if the child pees straight like a boy.

I hadn't yet thought it could be a girl. She opened her mouth several times and she whispered the name softly in front of her like a song tune. As he progressed he lost his somewhat abrupt roughness. He became Yan and like that he looked a bit like Iacq; and then it was even sweeter. She called him Yantje. It dragged through the air like a little wounded cry of a bird; it took flight and paled high and joyful like the summer wind. I would have rather shouted it like the jays with the pride of my lungs. Then she fell silent, she seemed, with her eyes fixed in front of her, to watch the name live and become a little man. I ceased to exist; there was only the child; and she was with him from the bottom of her life, with a great dream in her eyes. She spoke to him like he was there behind the door, moving her bright little hands. Madly she said to him:

- Ah! ah! you can laugh when I say Yantje! He already knows his name!

I suddenly stopped loving this little one.

The great pain came with the summer moon. She languishes for a whole day and then again at night, pressing her side with both hands. And finally her cries rose, so horrible that I would have given my blood not to hear them any more.

She was still shouting:

- Take the ax, kill me.

Why had the Old Man taught me to love life? Now I was going to the threshold and I held my fist up to the sky, I cursed someone up there; he too in the city was constantly blasphemed by the pain of men. And then this thing happened: I, the vomited child of mankind, the little old man given birth at the corner of a terminal, I thought pitifully of the sufferings of the unknown woman who had carried me. In the terrible night, for the first time my heart suddenly cried out to the one who had cursed me. A mother was born from my very tender and deep pity: the orphan, the hated offspring gave birth to his mother.

There are such powerful movements in nature that have no name! Perhaps it could have been called forgiveness, and she never knew it.

Dawn passed with its twitching shiver; a new day arose; and a little thing rolled in the bed of ferns. I was on my knees, leaning over the child, trembling all over my body, with the shock and fear of this life which was now stirring there and had come out of me. He let out his wild little yelp; the trees recognized the son of man; and Iule's agony was loosed. She sighed weakly:

- Go to the stream, get some water: we'll wash it together.

It had been so long since that woman's voice had spoken to me!

- O dear Iule! it seems to me that you too have just been reborn, I cried.

I laughed and cried with the convulsed face of a delirious man. And I hardly dared to touch her with my hands: she was much more sacred to me with her wound than on the day when the roses had bled for the first time. And there you have it, now they had fruited like the flower of the rose hips.

I went to the stream, brought back a bowl full of water. She herself had delivered the child from her hands, and she was holding it leaning against her breast, drinking the milk greedily. No one had taught them that; As soon as a baby has come to a mother among the animals, she lies down and he takes her udder; and life is the same everywhere. The child emptied the breast and then, holding it in her knees, she showered it with cool water. I went outside, exhausted, feeling the urge to embrace a living being against my chest. I would have liked to cry like the child. And, as there were only trees there, I opened my arms. I remained sobbing for a long time, my face glued to the rough bark of an elm tree; I thought I embraced the whole forest. Then a voice from afar called to me. A step quickly crossed the thickets. And I say:

- Dad ! dad ! the child has come!

The whole earth had to hear it: my heart was too small to contain such joy. And he was beside me, with his gray beard on my shoulder, weeping also softly:

- There, yes, the time has come: its cry has gone louder than the cries of jays. I heard it from the depths of the forest. And now you have a son, you who did not have a father.

We walked in the rising light. He took the child in his big hands, lifted it up to the light of the sky, and then he began to blow on his eyes as he had done for me one day. And religiously, three times in the silence of the forest, he said:

- Be John! Be a man ! Be the life!

A mystery hovered, a pause of eternity on the small naked flesh which wanted to take its share of humanity. It seemed that the souls of ancient men too had come from everywhere to this meeting of life. And I, with my mute mouth, was stirred in my fibers with deep turmoil, thinking that my race and the race of Iule had melted into the young blood of the child.

He had never finished gorging himself on milk; her mouth was a ring on Iule's breast. This was my little foal in the wild forest of my young strength. When he cried, my heart neighed with joy; my whole life was kicking with its little feet hitting the void. He was red like foxes. Iule flowed it into the stream and then she stretched it naked on the moss: the hot wind dried the wetness of her skin. The adventure through the forest, the wandering and amazed mornings began again. She carried it suspended by braided fibers from her shoulder; he slept behind his back, his shaken sleeps; and like the family of the first men, we went before us, singing and whistling with the birds. In the evening she would put him to bed near her in the bed of her hair.

Its substance prolonged ours and it was no different from the free growth of essences around us: it was the highest point of life among the elementary forms nourished with green sap. He made new gestures; to each one, I felt humanity rise; all together were as beautiful as the birth of a thought. I believed, in my simplicity, that they were playing with her little inner soul, descended to limits. You, O Iule, you watched the moon turn at the end of her little hands in the evening, like a ball.

He played with his feet, he dragged himself on his stomach after his shadow. The first step he took pushed the boundaries of the universe. There, in the city, they also have children and they don't see them growing up. A day and a day are not alike. Each dawn is a birth for the world and a hair that comes with beauty full of life.

There was about me this word of the ancestor: "Open your eyes and you will see." There, I tried to open my eyes as the child opened his hands to the sun, to the wind, to the shivering of the leaves.

Iule carrying her light weight between her shoulders, we went with the Father to harvest the officinal plants. That summer the harvest was plentiful; the bread we gave him in exchange fed us a lot. It was a great treat for us to think that we would never miss bread as long as the summer made the new shoots green again. The sacred sense of the eternity of the earth was thus revealed to us and associated with our destinies. Earth ! it was only a word, and it stirred us, it made a wind around us like a door opening onto something infinite. Just saying it, I was quite pale, with a shiver.

One day he told us:

- This forest is big; by walking for days, one only touches the limits; and then it is the sea and over the sea there is only the sky.

- What does he want to talk about? said Iule, stopping breastfeeding the child.

In my turn I say:

- I assure you, Father, we do not understand you. This is something that no one has ever told us about. She was not in the almanac.

With a stone he drew the shape of the continents on the ground; the great waters formed around a liquid ring; and the earth and the seas moved in space. However, together they were only an infinitely small point in the universe and the planets which shone in the night were also worlds where, no doubt, other men lived. Iule, with the little one in her arms, had bent her knees and was leaning over the signs he was making. She shook her head.

- When you would tell me that a hundred times, she said, there is something here that I will never understand.

She kissed the child and then laughed.

- You see, little man, one day you will be great; I will then also take a stone as he does and then I will tell you: this is the sea and this is the earth, and this is the sky. I'll see what you think of it.

But I, with my deep eyes, couldn't tear myself away from the sight of the circles. My heart was beating painfully. A heavy weight weighed me down as if the whole universe had weighed on my shoulders. And I couldn't think of anything to say, with a force chained inside me.

"Repeat the lesson again," I asked.

He picked up the pebble and only then was one thing in my life loosened; I took my head in my hands and cried like a little child.

The following days, I went alone in the forest and with a stick between my fingers, I drew the three circles of earth, water, space. I was no longer happy.

- There, I said to this man, now I must go before me through the world. If Iule wants to stay here with the little one, she can. I will go alone.

His voice trembled: he had the weakness of old men.

- I loved you like my son. You will not find better bread or more fruit elsewhere. Also consider that you will meet the men on your way.

- I'll take my ax.

So he gently shrugged his shoulders.

- Well, go, he said. We don't stop life.

I called Iule: she had put the child on the moss and was picking blackberries from the bramble tree, because once again we were approaching the end of summer. And when she had come, I said to her:

- Here ; we do not stop life. I'll go to the sea over there. If you prefer to stay here with the little one, you can.

She was under her yellow horsehair like a fiery sound. And she cried:

- I won't let you go alone. I will go with you, carrying the child. You will not take one step unless I take another with you.

Turning to the old man, I saw him leaning towards the ground and sorting the seeds he had gathered. With his calm forehead and clear eyes, he looked like a sage withdrawing from human actions. My heart softened, I put my hand on her shoulder and said to her sadly:

- So you will stay alone in the forest?

He replied quietly:

- I lived there alone before you.

We were silent, like two men looking at each other from an opposite shore. He picked up the seeds, straightened up, took a few steps, and then stopping, he shouted to me:

- We will travel together through the forest; while I will stop at the convent, you will continue your journey alone.

The next day, at dawn, we left the house; he was waiting for us near the hives; he had tied honey cakes and bread for us in his sack. He also gave Iule some clothes, saying:

- Men must not laugh at your nudity.

The forest closed in on us. When the child cried, Iule put her breast in her mouth; and then he would fall asleep, she would carry him suspended between her shoulders by lianas. The Old Man went ahead, clearing the way; Iule walked between us. I followed her, the ax slipped through my belt.

First, slight curves undulated. Day fell as we reached a mighty rock, arched open at its base.

- Here, said the Father, ancient men lived.

Never had my heart beat so strongly. In my turn, as they had done, I wanted to penetrate the rock; the cavity became less frequent; a dimmed light outlined its walls and then died. It seemed to me that I myself was forever separated from the living. I called Iule, shouting; his voice guided me to the exit. I appeared in the daylight, quite pale from having seen old humanity in the night of origins.

We spread a litter of leaves. Our deep voices roared under the vault like the sound of centuries. The air was dead and icy: I went to pick up some dry branches; I beat the flint. Our shadows with the flame lengthened to the limits of the den. Sometimes the Old Man advanced towards the bottom: his steps seemed to sink into the spirals of a well. When he returned, his waist seemed to stand out of time.

We slept all that night close to the heart of a tender and fierce humanity. She too, in her relentless march, knew the stage there and she waited for the day to come. Foxes yelped bitterly outside; wild cats were fighting; the harsh rattle of the great nocturnal birds did not cease.

And then the flights of rooks croaked: we knew that morning had come down.

New slopes became steeper; an eagle hovered for a long time. That one I couldn't have shot with my arrows. This volcanic earth then gradually flattens out. The caravan plunged into the pine forest: it extended for leagues; their nerve fibers alone had been able to grow in the light and ashy soil which the salty waters of the sea had once exhausted. The amused cries of the child could still be heard and Iule sang; his songs were sweet and made no sense. Sometimes she also whistled, imitating birdsong. The Father and I now walked in front without saying anything, with a heavy heart, for the time of separation was near.

He kissed me and said:

- Going straight ahead, you cannot fail to meet the sea. As for me, my path is to the east. Farewell !

He hugged me one last time in his chest; and striking the soft earth with his stick, he strode along. Iule had stayed behind with the child; he seemed to have forgotten her. I watched him advance under the trees, thinking: As long as you can see him, he will be alive for you; but who can say that then you will never see him again?

He was only a shadow; and now Iule had joined me: she was elf with the child and she hardly noticed that he had left us.

- See, I said, this man is gone and again we are alone as on the first day.

- Why also, she replied sourly, did you want to see this sea? Haven't you had enough of the stream? And are you sure that once we get there we will reach the limits of the world and then there will be nothing but emptiness?

The worry disappeared; I thought only of laughing at her conception of the earth. With the handle of my ax on the ground a large circle, I explained:

- The world is a ball, so understand. And who ever managed to find the end of a ball?

She shook her head and began to sing.

On the morning of the third day, we heard a huge rumor. We were advancing with difficulty in the soft desert of sands; cones ran; we reached the crest of it and I did not utter a cry. I was there like a man in astonishment considering the enormous sway of the waters. I no longer knew if I was alive; I felt no sense of grandeur or beauty.

Iule beside me laughed, said that after all it was only water; and she had believed her taller.

The powerfully curving tide swelled, pushing shells towards our feet. Iule would pick them up, put them in the light, and she made them into pendants, the clear noise of which tickled her ears.

Suddenly a sailboat plowed the open sea. I, who had hitherto remained silent, then uttered a savage cry; for now, with that small clear spot of the sails in the enormous void, the expanse was revealed to me. I had also cried under the tall foliage. Once again my temples in front of the prodigy cracked. The whole earth weighed so heavily on my shoulders that I fell on my knees. Iule picked up the shells by handfuls and let them fall back in rain to amuse the child. Her laugh, too, sounded like a seashell to her mouth.

The sailboat was no more than a bird in space; I was thinking of the sailors who, with this frail deck beneath them, risked themselves over the abysses. These were men made like me, with souls and limbs like mine; but I could hardly call myself a man compared to their great quiet heroism. Perhaps they were setting out to discover a world. My being was excited, humble and fraternal. I would have liked to hug them or just touch their clothes with my hands. Now the sea was small beside the man standing on a ship.

The clear point further diminished: I ran along the beach, I climbed the highest dune, with the desire to see it longer. He plunged into the horizon and again there was nothing but the enormity of the waters. My heart was beating forcefully. I returned to Iule, my teeth clenched on dark things in me. I had rather disdain for this animal creature who always laughed with the child. I loved them both with all my heart, but there it was, I was over there with the great vessel plowing the sea and I could hardly see them again, very small, on a tiny point of land.

With the sound and the dizziness of the sea in my head, I did not see a woman, only waving her hands, stirring light and music around the young charmed life of her infant. She does a simple and necessary thing like the sea itself by pushing her shells along the beach.

We went then, in the golden afternoon. The salts in the air shone like crystals. Iule broke a corner of the honey cake; and we had not exhausted all the fruits gathered in the forest. But suddenly with a large wave the sea rose, and she began to run, moaning, the little one in her arms. I too cried in my anger, believing that the sea was going to reach us. From a distance we watched her coming; she was leaping like a million raging beasts and she was terrible. If only she had climbed the mountains of sand, all the earth would have been crossed with one of her waves; and not a tree, the livid death of the sands, ad infinitum.

Iule's breast dried up with anguish; she lamented after the good forest, cried like a wounded beast and madly kissed the little life rolled up in her hair.

A great wind blew; night had fallen. The whole expanse was black as if the day would never rise again. And I, in this terror, I was speechless, listening to death bark. The maternal soul, the heroic and savage soul of the races then cried out.

- Save the child, she said, run in front of you to the forest, climb to the top of a large tree.

Having gone one last time to the waters, I saw that they had stopped.

The wind from the forest also sometimes seemed to roll the whole sky and then there was always a barrier that broke its strength. I touched my forehead with my fingers, like a man waking up from a horrible sleep. An immense hope softens me, a confidence in the goodness of nature. I was there trembling with all my body, with words in me like the waves of the sea. I had the infinite feeling of a deliverance as if now I felt myself in the big hands which at their pleasure unleashed and restrained the terrible sea. Iule! Iule! Here soon is the day and the sea recedes!

Step by step I advanced, pushing back the pack of pale dogs, entering the abyss with my bare chest, me defenseless, almost the equal of the men who split the abyss with their ship. Always a little more free land came out of the water. And Iule de la dune also watched the sea sink into its howling dwellings.

I dug a deep hole with the ax. The sand there was light and soft as down. She lay there, at the end of her bravery and agony, supporting the child with the fiery throbbing of her throat. Then I sat for a long time in the night, my eyes fixed on the ever farther bar of the waters. I was without ideas: yet at the bottom of my being something violently stirred, the dull force of a thought. There is a law, Little Old Man, there is a harmony which regulates everything and to which everything remains subject. There you are, yes, I believe it was that which rose and stirred in me like the sea itself. And at last the east quivered under the clear clouds, and the day had come once more.

We slept in the salty coolness of the dune. Peace and security were upon us. A young humanity thus went towards the unknown horror and having seen the sea coming down again, fell asleep quietly in the rocking waters. We had returned to the child days of the world; the feverish pulse of the storm had rumbled through us and now, beside the harmonious palpitation of the wave, we rested without fear. Iule was lying on my chest and her chest curved up in a cradle around the child's sleep. With my hands, I covered them both. Above us was the great blue softness of the air.

When I opened my eyes, the livid dogs again slowly came up. A mad pride swelled me; I went down screaming towards the sea. The waters leapt at my hocks, they spurted up to my loins, and I, a simple man of nature, I was already playing with their mysterious power. I took the child, I plunged him naked in the salts; the whole sea of one time passed, and then with that little life above my head, I was there like a man in sacred joy.

"See," I cried, "that too is a man. He and I have conquered death.

The sea was high. I entered the sands with Iule and held her there under my love. I had her in her deep life as if the sea and all the beauty and all the horror, I embraced them through her. I had not known this sublime sensation in the gentle murmur of the spring and the wind. A heart always equals the measure of the things around it. Now the violent sea had come up over me; I was a man who shuddered at having faced the Forces. There, he spent in this moment of love the eternity that there is in the silence and the crash of the sea. However then I was still only a creature of wild instinct.

In the evening, the sun rolled red: it seemed to dive lower than the horizon, drawn by the abyss. The whole sky smoked like embers under damp rags. And almost immediately great darkness reigned, the void howling from the depths. We had climbed to the highest dune to see the light longer, standing above the swells of gold and blood. Over there, the right bar of the waters, in a vertiginous retreat, this time appeared to us the end of the world. Yes, we were on this hill like the first humans ever to watch the death of the day sink into a cataclysm. Anguish to the point of stupor gripped our mute souls. The night was a deliverance for us; it flowed in a wave heavier than the sea. And now the entire beach was endlessly surrounded by little living lights.

Iule and I with our feet we stirred this fiery water. Our belt dripped with a tunic of jewels. We kissed each other with mouths like flaming fish. And I, innocently, said to him:

- Little Iule, don't you think these are pieces of the sun that have fallen into the sea?

The next day we walked part of the day ahead of us. No living being, no doubt, had been there. We lost hope of ever seeing a human face again. We were not sad, we felt rather the pride of having discovered a corner of the world. This was also the feeling with which I had come to the forest: it appeared to us now a tiny point of the universe beside the vast sea. Sometimes we ate the flesh of the shells; their taste left us with a burning freshness. Soon we were tortured by thirst: our kisses were salty like the air and the wind. The rest of the day we wandered, hoping for some fresh water. The evening grew cooler; we drank the night dew from our skins. But the next morning it rained: we collected the precious drops in our hands.

Another day passed and in my turn I began to cry within myself the forest and the old friend. I no longer liked the sea; a fearful weight of loneliness crushed me. However, I didn't think of going back. A force was pushing me, my face stretched out towards the waters, like my destiny. This was a great mystery.

As the fifth day fell, as we were sitting in the dune, the wind suddenly shouted human voices. My heart leaped: it had leaped like this every time the men had appeared. I took my ax and climbed to the point of the dunes. There were ten of them, their foreheads fierce. And Iule, beside me, was holding the child in his arms. Seeing us half-naked under our rags, they thought we had been stranded on the coast, after a shipwreck. First they stopped, astonished, defiant; and then they started running towards us with great clamor.

"Tell us where the money is," they shouted.

Their language was harsh, with consonants hissing and abrupt like the wind. I didn't know what money they wanted to talk about.

I took Iule in my arms. I was not afraid. If any of them had laid a hand on her or on Yantje, I would have brought him down with my ax. I say to them without anger:

- See, we're people like you. We come from the forest. There were only birds, trees and grasses there. We didn't hurt anyone.

They roamed the dune for a little while, like scenting dogs. And then coming back to us again, they shouted savagely:

- This land is ours!

- There, I said to them, if someone comes too close, I will strike him between the eyes with the ax.

They stepped back a little distance and between them they laughed at Iule's nakedness. Immediately I felt a great shame because of her. I had not experienced this feeling in front of the old man. I walked over to the one who appeared to be the oldest and quietly said:

- Give me a piece of your clothes to cover this one. In the forest we went naked and no one looked at us. Then, if you want, I will fight with one of you.

I spoke there like an ancient man come down from the mountains to the rivers. He too had confided in the idea that force alone decided the rank of beings.

The man measured me with his eyes and scorned my arms, which were less muscular than his. He did not know that I had seen the great sailors with childish and heroic hearts pass in the clouds, off the sea. So he shook his heavy shoulders and, turning to the others, he said, laughing:

- The boy has his ax and we only have our fists. This is not what would scare us either.

Immediately I threw down the ax, saying:

- Go pick it up.

One of them then stood up, came to put his shoulder against mine, and his head was sticking out of my head.

- Who are you, you so small, he said, to speak to us so boldly?

I was upright on my toes, lifting my forehead high. I say :

- Iacq was taller than you and I didn't tremble. I know the secrets of life.

Again they looked at each other, not understanding; and I suddenly felt that I was wearing something between my temples that made me taller above them all. The man says:

- Well, go your way together, you and that one. We won't hurt you. No one yet has looked us straight in the eye like you do, we who are dreaded sea-going men.

They sank into the dune and Iule was now quietly breastfeeding the child. But from afar they continued to look at us and after a while they came back.

- Listen, said the old man, there are sick women and children over there in our houses. If you want, you will come to live with us.

Their eyes were fierce and benevolent, and he spoke sincerely. The book suddenly beat against my chest; it throbbed like my very life. I say to Iule:

- If you believe me, we'll follow these men.

In the old days I would have thrown the pebble in the air.

She looked with a sigh in the direction where we had come, with regret for the forest left behind and she said:

- Where you go, I'll go.

We walked across the dune. I had given the ax to one of the men, he was carrying it on his shoulder. I felt much stronger with my bare hands. In a fold of the sands, a miserable hamlet at last appeared. A little girl threw a stone at us; women were turned towards the sea and shouted insults at us.

The men would simply say to them:

- This one knows the secrets.

What was there in common between these people and us? We had come through the forest like a king and a queen, rich in springs and wind and birds, in our happy young nakedness. On the contrary, great distress was upon them, all rough and puny, with sad eyes, eaten by salt. They brought before me two of their wives who were gnawing at a terrible disease, and now they were all around me, shouting with great pity:

- You who know the secrets, heal them.

My heart was then deeply moved, seeing that they had misunderstood my strength: I only knew the good grass of the forest.

- No, no, I cried with real pain, I can't. The beasts of the sea are in them. They should be taken there where there are grasses and stream water.

The revolt roared. The man who had measured her shoulder to mine took a step.

- Why were you telling us about secrets if you can't help them?

I replied fiercely:

- When a tree is rotten in its pith, all you have to do is drop it.

One of the mothers came in her turn, carrying her son, already almost a man, in her arms.

- Oh ! she moaned, cure him for me. He was not ten years old when the pain was already in his legs and he no longer walks. Think about all the tears that I have cried.

Powers immediately awoke in the unknown of my life. There came such a great surge of love that the waters gushed out of my eyes. I would have been told: "This young man will never walk again; I would have replied that he only had to put one foot in front of the other to go down the path. My mouth trembled, with that word to my teeth, and yet I stood there still motionless and mute, bound in my will.

I'm going to say something only a few will believe: it happened so simply that I wasn't surprised myself. I looked this boy in the eye, hugged him with all my might, and he was standing on his feet. I didn't know what I was doing. But this I did naturally as if I had always done it. I said to him deeply:

- Now I want you to walk.

He took three steps without his mother's help and in the great silence we could hear the sea rising towards the dune.

- Go, I said again, since you are healed.

And again, he was going as I said.

Only then did the woman's sobs resound: she led him by the arm, all shaken by wordless cries. And with her heart on the ground, she walked alongside and seemed to level the sands. The others now touched me with the tips of their hands. The whole hamlet came when the miracle was announced: they watched the boy with small steps advancing towards the waters. The mother cried:

- Don't go too far, son, you might not come back.

I, the poor boy of the towns, with my will alone had done this thing. My heart was lifted, I said to the paralyzed child: Walk! And he had obeyed my gesture. I was, however, simple and naked like them. But these were of my race of misery through time and because of that a great force of love had come to me. These rough souls now were gentle and submissive in my hands. We had a roof.

Every day they left to collect the wrecks that the flood threw up along the sands. When the sky and the sea darkened, they climbed to the top of the dunes to watch for shipwrecks. Formerly, they had had boats. One after another, they had been carried away, along with those who were riding them; they had two left, which they used to fish along the coasts. In the evening, in front of the doors, the oldest man recited wonderful stories. Well two hundred years ago they were a dreaded people. They had golden houses where people used to feast around the tables. Three times the sea had passed and twice they rebuilt rich mansions. The third time, there were only a few men left. These had gone to steal women from afar. But the times had come to an end:

In the town from which we came, one would have called this hamlet a collection of bandits. They didn't seem to care more about a man's life than they did about their own. Their fathers had been sea skimmers and, in turn, they lived on plunder, by chance of storms and shipwrecks. With my will upright between my temples, I thought: If at your command he who could not walk began to run, it is not more difficult for you to stretch out your hand over those rough hearts and lead them there. where they need to go.

The old almanac was still beating on my chest. I opened it to a page and then, sitting next to them in the dune, I went to the end of the page. I was amazed at all that was good and eternal in it. Perhaps only one man had written it and he had written it for all men. A small patch of land, depending on the rain and the wind, is enough to grow tall and durable species.

When I closed the yellowed sheets, they would tell me:

- Yes, that's fine, the book is right.

The ax hung on the wall, rusty from the sea air.

As they had neither arts nor industries, Iule taught them to weave baskets. I helped them repair their ruined roofs. With the stranded woods, they built fences for themselves. I went with the young men to the dune, I said to them:

- One day I'll take you to the forest. She came out of an acorn. You will plant one of the acorns and there will come to you a forest too.

Having stamped my foot on the ground, I said again:

- With this land, you will make houses.

I spoke like a man who dreams of populating a desert.

A winter thus passed: the sea entered the dune; boats ran aground on the coast; and they were wild again. Once, they rushed on the castaways: the murder hovered; and I, with the book in my hands, submitted them: I had told the paralytic to walk before him. And then the light mornings turned blue. Iule, stroking my young beard, spoke of the forest again. I stopped looking at the sea and in my turn felt infinite pain.

- Yes, I say as if in a dream, the new swarms have built new cities.

Flights of bees whirled around. The ages were filled with their toil and they worked for the ages. My new soul stirred in me: like them, I had come to the limits of the sea towards the flowers of harsh humanity and now I was laying the foundations of a city in the sands until then uncultivated. I no longer knew that Iule was there with his hands in my beard and his pale eyes looking towards the forest.

- Believe me, she said, we will go with the child. It has been so long since we drank the clear water from the stream.

My heart proudly rose and I replied:

- Woman, look at these men: they put their trust in me. Can I abandon them?

She took her head in her hands and softly moaned:

- When we lived together in the forest, there was no one between you and me.

So I pushed her away, shouting:

- Don't touch my strength. You, you dance with the child in the sun and you believe that the whole world fits in the little shadow that turns around you.

His arms unfolded; for a little while her belly as the tide had risen again; and she was very beautiful. So she came and leaned over, her arms heavy on my shoulder.

"The day you took me for the first time, you wouldn't have spoken to me like that," she said.

Feeling his side weigh heavily, I felt that his love had rights older than the others; for she was the first to come with me by the forest path. She held my life in the palm of her hands and my whole race endlessly passed away.

- I will always be a man to you that others will not have known, Iule. This I tell you sincerely.

She was laughing now like a little goat with her lip high.

Iule gave me a second male child towards the end of the summer, and the eldest was already running straight through the sands. My life ascended, stood before me like a people. I held this little flesh in my hands, and the whole earth was light beside it. I felt both a great force of pride and humility. Wasn't that also a miracle like the seasons, like the tree that comes out of a beech, like the enormous weight of the sea? However, a drop of my living substance had sufficed for me; all eternity had cried out in the child's first cry and my will had nothing to do with it.

The following spring we set out with the spades. The earth split, the ovens burned; they began to build houses. They always spoke of a great tower among themselves. Perhaps one day the sailors passing offshore would see fires there which would lead them towards a port; but there you have it, wood was lacking and they too were talking to me about the forest. I was saying :

- All the sea does not rise with a wave.

Iule, in the evening of the dunes, sang softly. She sang the green heart of loneliness and the song of warm waters. His eyes were religious, softened by a mystery. They listened to him moved and serious, with naive faith. The dream, the sweetness of life far from the salty shores awoke. They throbbed with longing for the lovely, cool earth beneath a light air. When they asked me if the time had not yet come to go and collect the acorns, I would go alone along the waters, weeping like a child. However, if anyone, at that moment, had tried to blow on my strength, perhaps I would have laid him low with my ax.

- If they know too soon the rest under the trees, I thought, they will never finish building the city.

It happened that these people living by the sea one day threw the spades there and, having walked towards me, said to me with frowning faces:

- There, we'll go there without you.

- Men of little faith, I replied, since when has it been written that the pastor will follow his flock? He alone knows the road and there are only herbs where he passes.

One of the elders weakly lamented:

- Do we have to die without our eyes, scorched by salt, being refreshed in the green light of the trees?

This one moved me because of his miserable years. His voice came to me as from the depths of agony.

I touched her eyelids with my fingers and said:

- Here are my hands on your wants, and my hands are life. Now life won't forsake you until you see the things promised. Believe what I'm telling you, life is with me.

A great force rose from the depths of my being: I held the life of this old man in my hands and I had spoken without deception, myself believing what I was saying to him.

- If so, said the others, let it be done according to your will. It is right that that one should order who has a sign on him.

So I was with these people like someone who came from the east. They were looking deeply at the life in my clear eyes. For having had it in me, I had deserved to be the shepherd who goes before the bleating of the flock. This one is closest to life which, without reasoning, puts one step in front of the other, and all bring closer to something that one does not know and which is destiny. I thought: One day there will come virgin and terrible men according to the heart of life and the earth will belong to them. A poor man like me who had been to tree and bird school had every right to think so.

The third summer burned down and the city rose. The forest then quivered in me again. It was the time when the helping vulnerable people ripened, when the wild bees distilled abundant honey. My heart swelled like the heart of the free sons of the earth once did at the idea of hot prey. At the fragrant limits, perhaps the Father was listening if footsteps did not come from the side of the sea.

I say to the men:

- Iule and I will go ahead, because now the time has come.

In the morning the waters sang. We walked for a whole day. When evening fell, we had reached the pine area.

At dawn, the tribe left; the air had lost its salty taste and smelled of resin. They picked up the cones, they ate the milky almonds. Our walk under the trees made the sound of heavy rain. Where we passed, the foliage was shaken as if by the wind, and then, in our footsteps, the immense peace of summer fell.

They went in line, mute, full of amazement, and sometimes they all cried out together in the intoxication of life. The height of the trunks frightened them; they thought they heard a heart beat underground; the crash of the sea was nothing compared to the noise of terrible eternity which rose from the depths of heavy silences. The old people had become children again: they stuck their ears to the bark and played with the sun on the road as with long golden insects. The sweetness of life made the eyes pale. I went in front as when we had left the sea: my hand, always in front of them, was raising barriers. And another day passed. We walked with the summer and the wind without haste, for now we were approaching the gardens of life. The youth of the world throbbed in us. I myself was a day of humanity,

The thick maze clears up. Wispy porches rose up; the enormous light thrill of the green centuries passed. One evening of ages fell on the last stage. Then the whole nocturnal forest stirred in me, the very pure joy of the origins. We had started from there in the morning of life and a destiny, after accomplished things, brought us back there, dragging after us the soul of a people. My clamor rose: I became again the savage chief who breathes his strength through the nostrils.

O Iule! now the dream led us by the hand. Our faces were recognized with mystery as on the first day: they were no longer the same as those which had looked at each other in front of the dark waters. You were really the age of the young marriage at the time of the halt in the spring night. My heart under your hand beat an eternity.

A humid, warm air perfumed the awakening. I led them towards the fresh water at the bottom of the ravine: they lapped it for a long time in the hollow of their hands. They had forgotten the acrid salt of the sea. It was there that the cave opened: I had seen rising there with the passing of the ages, the man of races. Sometimes all together uttered a tender savage clamor. They licked the sweet aromas from their mouths. And a new day of life dawned.

- Think then, I said to Iule, the same light wind which stirs the leaves above us is passing at this moment in the enclosure of the Father. Maybe he's already gone to visit the beehives.

I had a fresh and filial soul; my voice was shaking.

We entered the region of fatty plants and flowers as tall as pastures. I revealed to them the essences, the seeds, the herbs of life as to myself they had been revealed. They began to gather a bountiful harvest, and then I said to them:

- You see us here, but you will look for us in vain later. We will have disappeared in the forest. However, don't lose confidence and keep collecting the good herbs. You will see us return on the fourth day after this one.

They came to the edge of the shore and watched us climb the slope until we ceased to be visible to them. The forest opened, the enchantment of the morning under the ruddy arches. I was holding Iule by the hand and she was carrying the little child; the one called Yantje was running in front of us. We walked slowly through the tender hour: sometimes, with the tip of my lips, I whistled like birds. The milk powerfully swelled the woman's breasts; the laughter of the sap and the wind buzzed in my temples. I pressed the cold of the leaves to my flesh. Madness rolled over me in the grass. However, I was no longer the same angry man who huffed like the stallion. My heart cried out in the virgin silence and my mouth was silent. All my blood was leaping and it made no more noise than a grass under its feet. I walked like a dizzy man, with a heavy and delicious weight on me: I could not have explained that. When I happened to think that before evening we would be at the old friend's hut, my breath stopped for a little while. I kept my eyes on the ground, watching if he hadn't been there before us. We shuddered at the thought of taking his long beard in our hands: perhaps it fell to his knees.

The cuckoo sang in the beautiful afternoon. A wheel of gold buzzed. O Iule! the bees ! The bees ! They came to us like frontiers and led us. You wanted to take one: it stung you and we noticed that they had become wild again. The forest was reddish.

Our feet ran, light; our hearts flew with the ruddy flies. I had to break branches to pass: they hit us in the face. A madness of life had grown around the enclosure and rippled like the sea. The tender peace of the evening was over the house. Slowly I clapped my hands calling him by his father's name and Iule with light cries excited the child.

- Laugh, little man! If he's already asleep, your laughter will wake him up.

There was such a deep silence there and the grasses were tall as trees.

Oh ! Oh ! was such a thing possible! He slept on the threshold an eternity of sleep: the clamor of a people could not have awakened him. He slept there like a century turned on the side where the sun goes. The end of the day had surprised him in his high chair of branches. The heavy hairs of his beard still hung from his chin and yet there was no longer a face: there was only the fermented residue of life. The jaws had fallen and remained open like the doors through which his soul had gone.

Dad ! O Father! very infinitely and only our Father! My blood froze horribly. My sobs were a dry harrow in my throat and I remained without a cry, with the low bark of a beast in my roots. I couldn't think, cry, or make any gesture, still watching with my dead eyes the bones turn green. O Father! there were nothing more than old bits of substance returned to nature! You, the ancestor of the forest, were now less than the smallest living insect; you were the inert hub of a swirling grindstone.

Iule slowly walked through the thicket of grass. I felt his breath on my cheek.

- See, she said, would you not believe that he lives?

I followed the gesture of his hand. A light passed. My eyelids were torn with pliers. And in my turn I saw the frightening and beautiful thing that a simple woman had seen before me. The beard trembled, moved with a quiver of life like water and like leaves. Moss fluffed the jawbones. A grass seed had sprouted from the eye sockets. And the slender stalk of a birch sprang up from the ground between the feet. A deep ivy, soft brambles had wrapped around the body and chained it with hairy ties to the chair. As one of the hands had remained on the knees, a bindweed seemed like a small candle in that hand, with its flower at the end like a flame.

The forest in the footsteps of death had entered and he slept there in a royal shroud of gold and emeralds. There, yes, all life, with a finger on its lips, had come. She had looked deep with empty eyes and then she had cleaned him from the stains of death, like a burial woman. She had woven him an immortal mantle of beautiful young essences. Now the house was green, the whole summer was laughing beyond the threshold. A shiver stirred in the skylight like the gesture of an arm. The cool heart of the forest throbbed in the place where a human heart had stopped. And then again I saw this: a bee passed, entered the bindweed, and in the corner of the door, an empty nest hung: the bird had made it with the hairs of the beard.

My tears flowed softly: they watered the earth which had drunk life and which had breathed life. They were not bitter: they resembled the ones I had poured whenever I had felt in the presence of the great mystery. Life ! Life ! Iule! My temples throbbed, an immense confidence lifted my being: we too were one of the waves which incessantly carried the soul of the world. He was standing in front of us, very gentle, with his child's eyes and he raised his hand, he spoke to us like the day he had taught us the eternity of all living things. His heart was pounding in the forest.

"So think about that, you," said Iule. Once he told us about the flowers and leaves that would come out of him. See: now all the bees have come.

The hives, in the evening, had a supreme murmur, and they whirled on the threshold like her ancient soul. So we stayed a long time without speaking, holding each other entwined in our love and continuing to gaze at the beauty of life, more beautiful when we emerge from death. A laughter arose from the earth near us: we did not know that the little child had come like bees and for play he held in his little hands the immense feet of the ancestor. This too was a symbol, like the bees and the green house and ourselves with the hot throbbing of our desire. She smiles.

"Come to the hut, to our place," she said.

The sky turns pale; a light wind blew; the young birch and the ivy shuddered, and night had entered: she put the bolt on the threshold. With his secret dead, in his peace of eternity, the Old One always seemed to keep the holes of his eyes open on the side of life. One day he had left the towns like us; already at that time he had died for men, and we did not know what destiny had made him savage and benevolent.

Now Yantje was asleep. I laid him on my shoulder and we went in front of us, walking through the tall vegetation: they had invaded the paths by which the old man came to meet us. The moon widened, but we could not find our home of young lovers. It seemed that she too had returned to nature. And I understood that the last link which attached me to the old life was thus broken and that I was irresistibly carried away towards a new life.

Iule said to me:

- Let's not go any further. There are ferns here.

Then the morning shook. She put my hand on her stomach and asked me if this time again I did not feel the stirring of life.

I held her pressed against me in the virgin day, and she was very great, august as the everlasting morning. There, my race had once again quivered. She was the tree of my life, with branches that would stretch through time.

The day was breaking. I thought of those who were waiting for me on the other side of the forest. The path brought us back to the enclosure; all the hives were awake; a cloud buzzed around our steps. In the light morning the house opened. The young summer of the forest had returned; all the birds were singing. A fresh life of eternity quivered in the bindweed and the birch.

I stood in the doorway for a moment with the tremor of my life in my hands. I did not disturb a branch or a leaf. I left the door open, and followed by Iule, I went to the men.

It was the evening of the fourth day. The wood closed around us as it had opened one morning and everyone came running, asking what I had seen.

- Life.

I wasn't saying anything else. I was like a man who came out of a cloud and saw a secret and eternal thing. But they looked at me with astonished and submissive eyes. Surely, they said to each other, a miracle has happened. He makes the gesture of someone above him in front of us. Yet there had only been the miracle of the wind and the little germinated seeds; there was the whole forest that had grown back with a bit of bone and blood where a son of old humanity had fallen asleep. But Iule went behind the trees mysteriously; I didn't know what she was saying; his words sounded like little pebbles falling into a well.

I raised my staff and brought them back towards the sea. There, I thought, you were naked and you are much more naked now: you no longer have even the shade and the light of the forest on your skin. A heavy sadness passed; and then the old almanac beat the heart of my life. Go ahead, man; humanity does not stop. Being with this people, you yourself are a people.

So Iule and I left the cool heart of the forest forever. I had followed my life: it had not followed me; and other things have happened since. I was the worker who had risen before dawn; I lived a great time of humanity and now there is a young city by the sea and free men. None of this would have happened if one morning I had not gone with Iule to the forest. Each man, with a personal and ingenuous soul, must start all life before him and I put my foot where the first ancestor put his. I asked for my sustenance from the land, I lived lonely in murder and innocence. I have raised my roof with my hands; my gods, I created them according to my destiny. And one day the tribes appeared: I said to those who were hungry: here is the bread; to those who died: this is life; to those who sank the boats: do not go against the wish of the storm. I gave them no laws: so they knew neither hypocrisy nor serfdom. But I helped them build a city; they had industries; living between the eternal sea and the forest, they have remained close to the forces, in the very heart of nature.

I turned the last leaf of the old book; my day is over: I can quietly wait for death. I know she is still one of the forms of life. I will therefore live in the ages like the ancestor in the living essences of the forest. A human forest will grow green again with my open arms beneath the earth and my bones will grow back through the races.

END

CPSIA information can be obtained
at www.ICGtesting.com
Printed in the USA
BVHW041444210922
647645BV00001B/49